D0935216

ANNEXE DE LA BIBLIOTHÈQUE
BIBLIOTHECA
uOttawa
LIBRARY ANNEX

SPATIAL VARIATION OF BLACK URBAN HOUSEHOLDS

David R. Meyer
University of Massachusetts

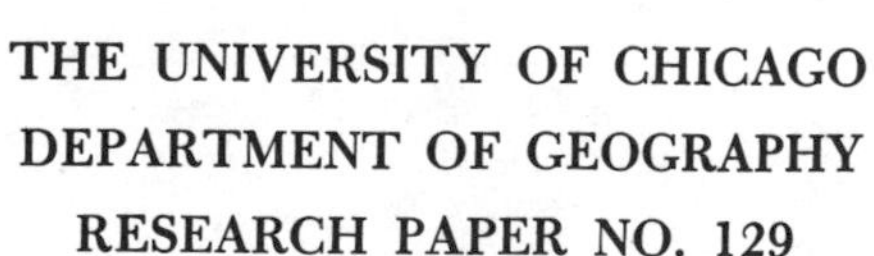

THE UNIVERSITY OF CHICAGO
DEPARTMENT OF GEOGRAPHY
RESEARCH PAPER NO. 129

1970

Published 1970 by The Department of Geography,
The University of Chicago, Printed by The University
of Chicago Printing Department, Chicago, Illinois

Library of Congress Catalog Card Number: 72-129455

Research Papers
The University of Chicago
Department of Geography
1101 E. 58th Street
Chicago, Illinois 60637

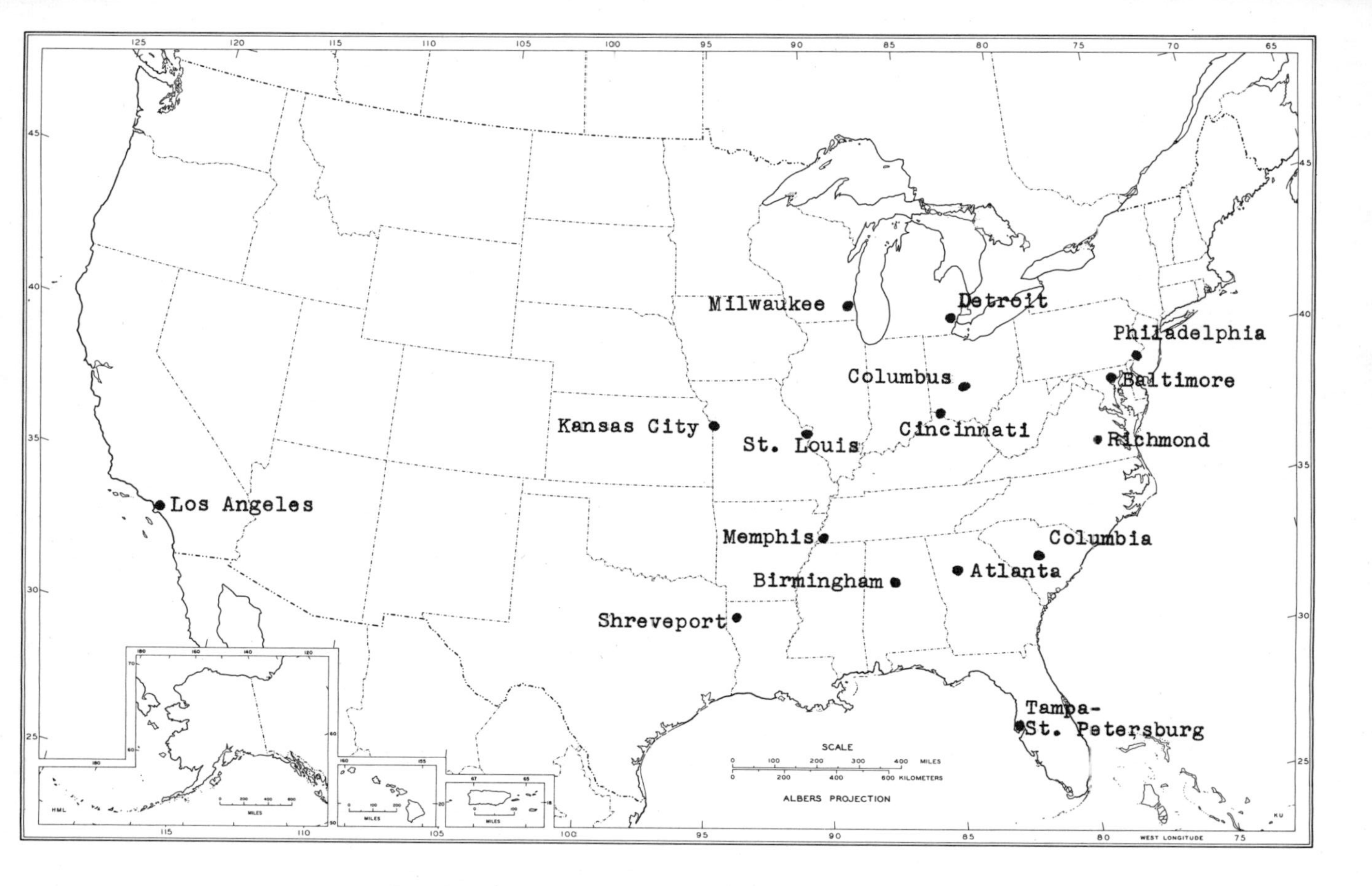

Location of Sixteen United States SMSA's Included in Study

ACKNOWLEDGMENTS

This investigation was supported in part by a grant from the Welfare Administration and Social Security Administration, U. S. Department of Health, Education, and Welfare, Washington, D. C.

I wish to thank Brian J. L. Berry for his encouragement and assistance in this study. Chauncy Harris provided helpful comments in the final stages of writing. I also appreciate the editorial assistance of my wife, Judy.

David R. Meyer

Amherst
August, 1970

TABLE OF CONTENTS

LIST OF TABLES

Table | Page

LIST OF ILLUSTRATIONS

Figure | Page

CHAPTER I

INTRODUCTION

In the United States the term "ghetto" is used to refer to that area of a city in which Afro-Americans live.[1] Connotations of the term are generally of a derogatory nature such as slum housing, crime, social disorganization, and poverty. Judging from the most common use of the term in the popular media and many scholarly articles, the ghetto is considered to be relatively undifferentiated in its internal spatial structure. This explicit or implicit characterization of the ghetto as an undifferentiated area of the city in the minds of many scholars may be one explanation for the lack of studies of the structure and patterns of black residential areas. Instead, the studies of black housing and black residential areas have tended to be focused on such topics as

1) the types of constraints on black housing choice, especially constraints encountered when Afro-Americans attempt to move into "white" neighborhoods,[2]

---

[1]Louis Wirth, based on his survey of the literature concerning the origin of the term "ghetto," concludes that the term seems to be of Italian origin and was used to refer to the Jewish quarter in European cities. See Louis Wirth, The Ghetto (first published Chicago: University of Chicago Press, 1928; Chicago: University of Chicago Press, Phoenix Books, 1956); pp. 1-3. Although Wirth employed the term to refer to a Jewish settlement in Chicago in his book, The Ghetto, the term has not continued to be used in the United States to refer to Jewish settlements in cities. Instead, the term "ghetto" has come to refer to that area of a city in which Afro-Americans live. Some studies which examine the origins of black ghettoes are: Gilbert Osofsky, Harlem: The Making of a Ghetto (first published New York: Harper & Row, 1966; New York: Harper & Row, Harper Torchbooks, 1968); Allan H. Spear, Black Chicago: The Making of a Negro Ghetto, 1890-1920 (Chicago: The University of Chicago Press, 1967); Robert C. Weaver, The Negro Ghetto (New York: Harcourt Brace & Co., 1948); and T. J. Woofter, Jr., ed., Negro Problems in Cities (Garden City, N. Y.: Doubleday, Doran & Co., 1928).

[2]The references concerning specific constraints on black residential choice are numerous. Some useful ones are: Nathan Glazer and Davis McEntire, eds., Studies in Housing and Minority Groups (Berkeley and Los Angeles: University of California Press, 1960); John M. Gries and James Ford, eds., Negro Housing, Report of the Committee on Negro Housing, The President's Conference on Home Building and Home Ownership (Washington, D.C.: National Capital Press, 1932); Charles Tilly, Wagner D. Jackson, and Barry Kay, Race and Residence in Wilmington, Delaware ([New York]: Bureau of Publications, Teachers College, Columbia University, 1965); and Weaver, The Negro Ghetto.

2) the changeover from white occupancy to black occupancy,[1]

3) the so-called "integrated" neighborhood,[2] or

4) comparisons of black housing with white housing.[3]

The above topics deal chiefly with that small fraction of black households who come into contact with the white housing market. However, we know very little about black residential choice within the black housing market and the consequences of these choices for the spatial differentiation of black households among black residential areas.[4]

The purpose of the present study is to examine the relationship between the spatial variation of black households and the spatial variation of housing in cities. The overriding hypothesis is that the spatial variation in the characteristics of housing among black residential areas is a significant element in the spatial variation of the characteristics of black households in cities.

Definitions and Terminology

Black residential choice

Residential choice refers to the whole complex of factors involved in deciding to move, examining alternatives, and making a final decision about relocation of the residence. The term choice is employed in the broad sense. It refers to the process of choosing among a set of possible alternatives and the choice which is constrained by factors such as income. More specifically, black residential choice refers to the residential choice process as it applies to Afro-American households.

---

[1]These studies revolve around the idea of invasion-succession. Some examples are Eleanor K. Caplan and Eleanor P. Wolf, "Factors Affecting Racial Change in Two Middle Income Housing Areas," Phylon, XXI (1960), 225-33; Otis D. Duncan and Beverly Duncan, The Negro Population of Chicago (Chicago: University of Chicago Press, 1957); E. F. Schietinger, "Racial Succession and Value of Small Residential Properties," American Sociological Review, XVI (December, 1951), 832-35; and Eleanor P. Wolf, "The Invasion-Succession Sequence as a Self-Fulfilling Prophecy," Journal of Social Issues, XIII, No. 4 (1957), 7-20.

[2]For example see Eunice Grier and George Grier, "Market Characteristics in Interracial Housing," Journal of Social Issues, XIII, No. 4 (1957), 50-59; and Henry G. Stetler, Racial Integration in Private Residential Neighborhoods in Connecticut (Hartford, Conn.: Commission on Civil Rights, 1957).

[3]Most studies of black housing deal only with the gross characteristics of housing. Their purpose is generally to make comparisons with white housing rather than study the black housing situation per se. A typical example of this type of study is Beverly Duncan and Philip M. Hauser, Housing a Metropolis--Chicago (Glencoe, Ill.: The Free Press, 1960), pp. 168-233.

[4]The terms black residential choice, black housing market, and black residential areas are defined in the next section.

Black housing market

Most black households make their residential choices within the black housing market. The black housing market includes all dwellings made available for occupancy by black households. Since white households rarely move into dwelling units previously occupied by black households, the black housing market is essentially a separate housing market from the white housing market.[1] The major contact of blacks with the white housing market is on the periphery of the black housing area where black households may replace white households. These dwelling units then become part of the black housing market.

Black residential areas

The black housing market can be divided spatially into black residential areas. For the purposes of this study a black residential area is arbitrarily defined as each census tract in a metropolitan area which has 400 or more nonwhites of whom at least 90 per cent must be Afro-Americans.[2] Of course some black residential areas will include whites within their boundaries. These will frequently occur in areas undergoing a change from white to black occupancy.

Theoretical Approach

Individual choice

At the level of individual choice it is generally recognized that the type of housing a household chooses depends upon the characteristics of the household. For example the higher the income of the household the more money the household spends on housing. If we assume for the moment that RENT per month is the money households spend on housing and INCOME is the household's yearly income we would therefore consider RENT to be the dependent variable and INCOME the independent variable, that is

$$\text{RENT} = f(\text{INCOME})$$

However, the focus of this study is not on the specific individual choices of black house-

---

[1]The writer simply appeals to the study by Karl E. Taeuber and Alma F. Taeuber, Negroes in Cities (Chicago: Aldine Publishing Company, 1965), in which they report extremely high segregation indexes for all cities in the United States. Since most black households do not live near white households, I believe we can safely assume that the segregation pattern is a reflection of separate black and white housing markets.

[2]The criterion of 400 nonwhites is used merely because the Census Bureau provides separate census tract data on nonwhites when there are at least 400 in a tract. The criterion of 90 per cent Afro-American is to insure that the data apply primarily to Afro-Americans. Since there are at least 400 nonwhites in each residential area I have essentially excluded all Afro-Americans who live within predominantly white residential areas.

holds with regards to housing. Rather it is concerned with the aggregate decisions of a set of households with regards to a particular spatial location, that is, the analysis involves an ecological study of aggregate choices within black residential areas.

Aggregations of individuals

At the individual household level households decide how much they want to pay for RENT. Once having decided the amount of RENT, the households must ultimately make a choice of a particular location of the housing to be purchased. After this choice has been made, the question arises as to how households will be distributed across the city by characteristics such as income. Will every residential area have the complete range of incomes and will there be substantial spatial differentiation? Since I assume that households choose housing with particular characteristics which are functions of the household's characteristics then I would expect that the spatial distribution of the characteristics of households would be related to the spatial distribution of the characteristics of housing, especially since black Americans often have no other choice but to buy from a fixed stock of housing rather than, like the white suburbanite, building new housing. I will generally assume in this study that the spatial distribution of housing characteristics is, as a result, outside the immediate control of the individual black household. Thus when the black household makes a decision about where to locate, it is confronted by an existing supply of housing distributed in a particular manner within the city. Furthermore, I assume that the only housing supply relevant to a black household is that which is already occupied by black households. I do not think this is too restrictive since I will be limiting myself to only one point in time, namely 1960, and since the analysis is ecological.

The level of spatial aggregation which I am employing in this study is the residential area which I have already defined. Each residential area is characterized by the type of housing contained in it. I am especially interested in those household decisions in which the housing characteristics are important factors in choosing a spatial location. Furthermore, I am interested in the preferences of households in terms of living near other types of households.

In most cases I will therefore be considering the characteristics of households occupying a residential area as being a function of the housing characteristics of that area. That is, the household characteristics will be considered the dependent variables and the housing characteristics the independent variables, or

Household Characteristics = f(Housing Characteristics)

As is evident, this is the reverse of the individual choice relation. Treating the household characteristics as being the dependent variables follows from my assuming that black households are faced by a fixed stock of housing and then asking, what will be the spatial distribution of households?

Necessary conditions for association between household and housing characteristics among residential areas

Two conditions are necessary for the existence of an association between household and housing characteristics among residential areas.

1. There are systematic regularities in individual residential choice such that, given the characteristics of a household, we can predict with reasonable degree of accuracy the type of housing[1] the household will choose.
2. Housing types of different kinds are not uniformly distributed among residential areas.

If neither condition were true, this would imply that individual choice was essentially random and housing was uniformly distributed among residential areas. In such a situation, an association between household and housing characteristics among residential areas could not occur. If condition 1 were true but condition 2 did not hold, this would imply regularities in individual choice but a uniform distribution of housing among residential areas. Therefore, all types of households would be represented in every residential area because each residential area had the complete range of housing characteristics. Again, no association between household and housing characteristics among residential areas could occur. Finally, if condition 1 did not hold but condition 2 were true, this would imply that there were no regularities in individual residential choice and housing was not uniformly distributed among residential areas. Without regularities in residential choice the distribution of households would be unrelated to the distribution of housing. Therefore I conclude that conditions 1 and 2 must hold simultaneously for an association to exist between household and housing characteristics among residential areas.

---

[1] I am using the term housing in a broad sense to refer to all of the characteristics of housing units such as value, size, condition, etc.

CHAPTER II

CONCEPTUAL FRAMEWORK

A Residential Choice Framework

A household derives a place utility from its residential location.[1] The place utility is a net composite of utilities which the household derives from its dwelling, neighborhood, and relative location with respect to the household's movement pattern. Thus the residential location is a comprehensive environment.[2] Expressed in a functional form,

$$PU = f(S,\ V,\ N,\ \ldots) \tag{1}$$

where PU is the place utility and S, V, N, etc., are various elements in the household's environment to which it attaches a positive or negative utility.

The set of place utilities which the household perceives and to which it responds is termed the action space.[3] Let us assume that the household ranks residential locations in its action space according to their perceived place utility. That is,

$$PU_{RL_{i+1}} > PU_{RL_i} \tag{2}$$

where PU is the place utility and the subscript RL_i refers to the ith residential location (RL). Then the action space can be expressed as a function. See Figure 1. I will call this function the location-utility function. Each point on the curve represents the place utility the household attaches to a particular residential location.

The level of aspiration (LA) on the place utility scale represents the level of place utility which the household wants to derive from its residential location, that is, it repre-

---

[1]The concept of place utility was introduced by Julian Wolpert. See Julian Wolpert, "Behavioral Aspects of the Decision to Migrate," Papers of the Regional Science Association, XV (1965), 161-63.

[2]The three components which comprise a household's environment were suggested by Lawrence A. Brown and Eric G. Moore in "The Intra-Urban Migration Process: A Perspective," Geografiska Annaler (forthcoming).

[3]Wolpert, "Behavioral Aspects of the Decision to Migrate," p. 163. Wolpert refers to the individual rather than the household, but otherwise this definition of action space is the same as Wolpert's. The idea of action space is borrowed from Kurt Lewin's concept of life space in Field Theory in Social Science (New York: Harper and Row, 1951).

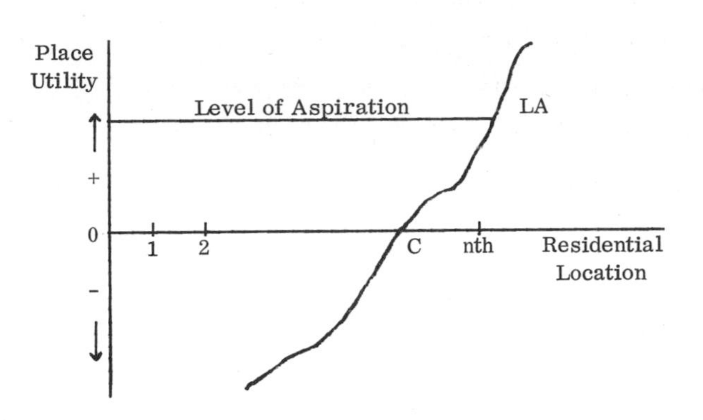

Fig. 1.--Location-Utility Function

sents a goal the household would like to achieve.[1] The lower bound on the level of aspiration is point C. C represents neutral place utility. Below C place utility is negative (dissatisfaction) and above C place utility is positive. It is conceivable that

$$LA = C = PU = 0 \quad (3)$$

That is, the household is indifferent to its residential location and has a zero level of aspiration. However, the case where LA is less than C is assumed to be impossible. No household desires a residential location with which it will be dissatisfied.[2] Thus

---

[1] The use of the concept level of aspiration in this discussion is partly based upon an article by Sidney Siegel, "Level of Aspiration and Decision Making," Psychological Review, LXIV (1957), 253-62. An alternative approach is taken by Lawrence A. Brown and Eric G. Moore. They use the concept of aspiration region rather than aspiration level. The aspiration region is bounded by two n-element vectors which represent the upper and lower limits of the set of n-dwelling criteria specified by the household. See Brown and Moore, "The Intra-Urban Migration Process: A Perspective." Undoubtedly their notion of aspiration region is more realistic than the use of level of aspiration. However, the concept level of aspiration is sufficient for the nature of my study.

[2] Some writers might prefer to have the level of aspiration be defined as a point separating positive and negative net utilities. For example see Wolpert, "Behavioral Aspects of the Decision to Migrate," pp. 161-62. The present writer feels that this may be unnecessarily restrictive. Hence in my discussion I do not restrict LA to be equal to neutral net utility.

$$LA \geq C \tag{4}$$

for all households.

In analyzing residential choice we are concerned with the difference between the level of aspiration (LA) of the household and the place utility the household derives from its actual residential location (PU_{RL}) at a given point in time. See Figure 2. I postulate that the probability of the household seeking a new residential location increases with increasing difference between LA and PU_{RL}. That is,

$$d = |LA - PU_{RL}| \tag{5}$$

and

$$Pr(M) = f(d) \tag{6}$$

where Pr(M) is the probability of moving. I assume that when d = 0, that is $LA = PU_{RL}$, then

$$Pr(M) = f(0) = 0 \tag{7}$$

Thus the probability of moving is zero when the place utility of the household is equal to its level of aspiration. Also, if $PU_{RL} > LA$ we assume that the probability of moving is zero. Equation 6 is illustrated in Figure 3.

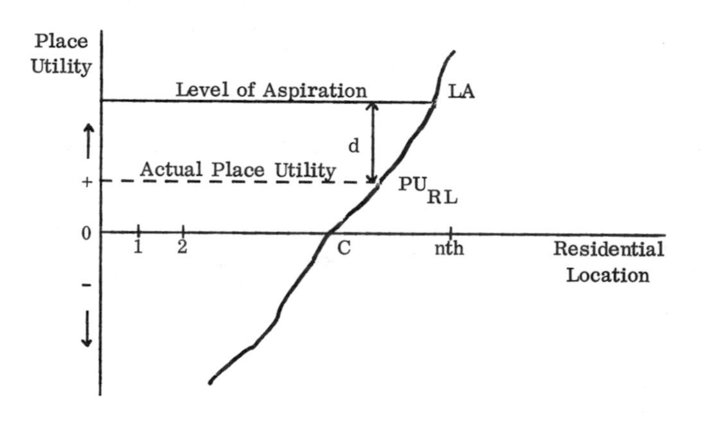

Fig. 2.--Level of Aspiration (LA) and the Place Utility of a Household at Its Residential Location (PU_{RL})

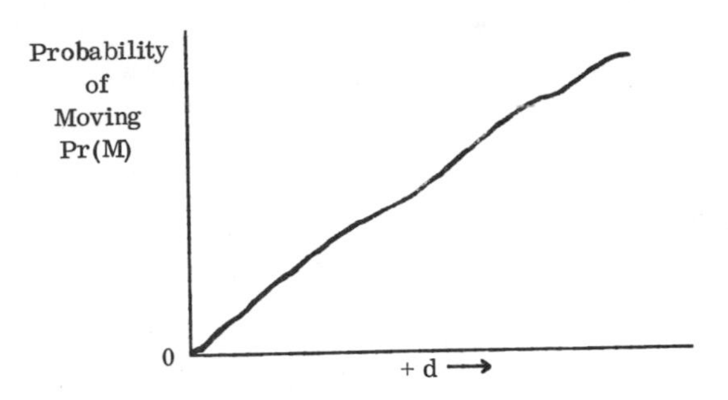

Fig. 3.--Probability of Moving as a Function of d

The framework which has been developed can be used to analyze the residential choice process. This process will be analyzed in two parts: (1) the decision to seek a new residence and (2) the search for and evaluation of alternative residential locations.[1]

The decision to seek a new residence

In discussing the decision to seek a new residence emphasis will be placed on isolating the changes in the relationship between the household's needs and its environment[2] which lead to an increase in the probability of a household making a decision to seek a new residence. Such increases in probability can arise from either a rise in the level of aspiration or a decline in the place utility a household derives from its residential location.[3] One simplifying assumption is made. The household's location-utility function is assumed

---

[1] The twofold division of the residential choice process is used in Brown and Moore, "The Intra-Urban Migration Process: A Perspective."

[2] As mentioned previously, environment includes the dwelling, neighborhood, and relative location with respect to the household movement patterns.

[3] These two possibilities illustrate the major points. Other combinations are also possible such as the level of aspiration increasing while the place utility declines or a greater increase in the level of aspiration than in place utility.

to be constant. Thus changes in the level of aspiration (LA) or place utility (PU_{RL}) involve a different perception, on the part of the household, of where its LA or PU_{RI} lie on the function.

Rise in the level of aspiration.--The effect of an increase in the level of aspiration holding place utility constant is shown in Figures 4 and 5. The increases in aspiration level can result from a variety of factors. For example, annual increases in the wage rate can cause a rise in the value of house which the household feels it can afford or make possible owning where only renting was feasible before.[1] The same effects can result from the wife entering the labor force.

A rise in the husband's occupational status also may raise the level of aspiration. A different house in a "better" neighborhood will become desirable. Changes in occupational status may occur by movement from one occupation to another of higher status or an individual may achieve a higher status within the same occupation. Thus changes in occupational status or social mobility may account for one move or as many as two or more moves in the lifetime of a household.[2]

Also, a desire for greater accessibility to entertainment facilities may raise the aspiration level of single men and women and thus increase the probability that they will move to different apartments.

Decline in place utility.--Holding level of aspiration constant, a decline in the place utility a household derives from its residential location will increase the probability of the household moving. See Figure 6 and refer back to Figure 5. Change in the life cycle[3] of the family is probably the most important factor in causing a decline in the place utility the household derives from its dwelling. Especially important are the changes in family size. Additional members such as a new child or relatives moving in can lead to

---

[1]James W. Simmons, "Changing Residence in the City: A Review of Intraurban Mobility," Geographical Review, LVIII (October, 1968), 632.

[2]In his review article, Simmons seems to downgrade the importance of social mobility in accounting for intra-urban mobility. At most one move of a household arises from social mobility, Simmons says in "Changing Residence in the City," p. 632. However, evidence from Blau and Duncan seems to indicate that intragenerational social mobility is not infrequent and hence may account for more than one move; see Peter M. Blau and Otis Dudley Duncan, The American Occupational Structure (New York: John Wiley & Sons, Inc., 1967), pp. 49-54.

[3]The term life cycle refers to characteristic stages of a family such as marriage, childbearing, childrearing, children leaving home, and final dissolution of the family. See Paul C. Glick, American Families (New York: John Wiley & Sons, Inc., 1957).

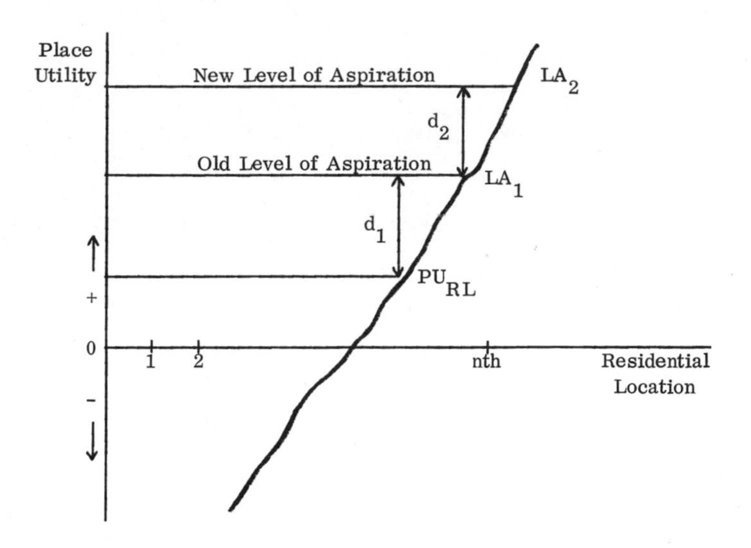

Fig. 4.--Increase in Level of Aspiration

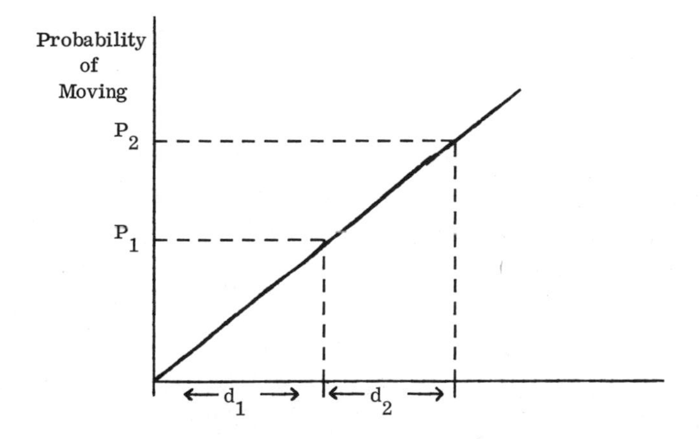

Fig. 5.--Increase in Probability of Moving

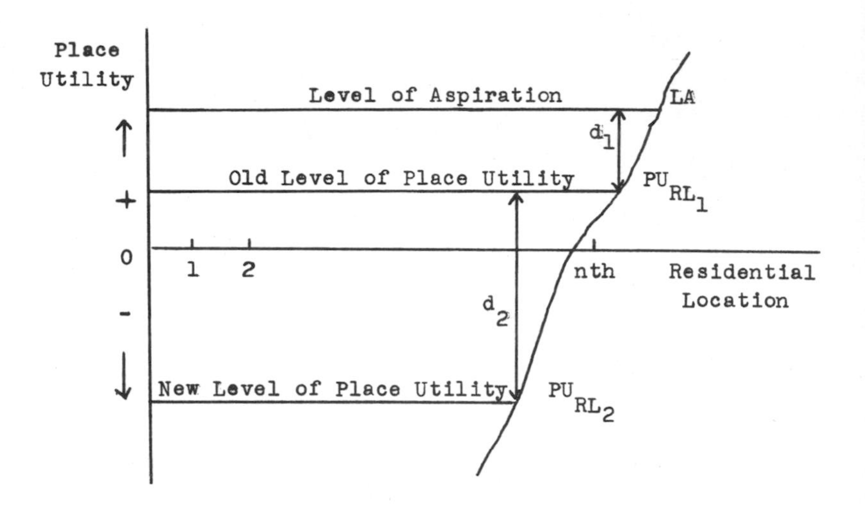

Fig. 6.--Decrease in Place Utility

perceived overcrowding and hence a decline in place utility.[1] The decline in size of household is probably less important in causing declines in place utility since too much space is not as serious as too little space.[2] Other factors such as deterioration in the dwelling also will cause declines in place utility. Neighborhood changes in the form of encroaching residential or commercial blight and ethnic or racial change can also cause a decline in the place utility of a household.

Probably the most significant alteration in the location of the household with respect to movement patterns occurs when the head of the household changes jobs. However, such a change may not be perceived in a negative fashion by the household.[3] Thus even if travel time and cost increase, the benefits derived from the new job may overshadow the transportation disutilities.

---

[1]Peter H. Rossi especially stresses the importance of the life cycle and dwelling size interaction in influencing mobility in Why Families Move (Glencoe, Ill.: The Free Press, 1955), p. 175.

[2]Eric G. Moore, "The Structure of Intra-Urban Movement Rates: An Ecological Model," Urban Studies, VI (February, 1969), 24.

[3]In his review article, Simmons claims that all studies have rejected job location as an important factor in intra-urban household movement. See Simmons, "Changing Residence in the City: A Review of Intraurban Mobility," p. 637.

Search for and evaluation of alternative residential locations

Assuming that a household has made a decision to move, the next step is to search for and evaluate alternative residential locations. We will consider search behavior very briefly[1] and focus instead on the evaluation of alternative residential locations.

In their review of literature on intra-urban activity patterns, Brown and Moore concluded that the information per unit area for a household will tend to exhibit distance-decay properties.[2] Such a pattern, coupled with the finding that most moves are short,[3] suggests that the search for new residential locations is predominantly carried out close to the household's current residential location.

The three components of the environment of a residential location provide a useful framework for analyzing the criteria the household applies when choosing a new residential location.

Dwelling characteristics.--Two criteria appear to be foremost in the household's evaluation. These are space requirements and cost considerations.[4]

Space requirements are different at various stages in the life cycle of the family. Single people, young childless couples, and elderly couples generally have the smallest space requirements. Families with children and/or relatives and nonrelatives in the household need more space.

The increase of ownership with increase in age and size of family[5] is also partly related to space requirements. Houses tend to have more interior space than apartments and they generally have yards which provide play space for the children.

---

[1]For a detailed discussion of search behavior see Brown and Moore, "The Intra-Urban Migration Process: A Perspective."

[2]Ibid.

[3]Simmons, "Changing Residence in the City: A Review of Intraurban Mobility," p. 640.

[4]Rossi, Why Families Move, p. 154. Rossi also found design requirements to be very important. However, consideration of design requirements is beyond the scope of my research.

[5]Sherman J. Maisel and Louis Winnick, "Family Housing Expenditures: Elusive Laws and Intrusive Variances," in Proceedings of the Conference on Consumption and Saving, ed. by Irwin Friend and Robert Jones (2 vols.; [Philadelphia]: University of Pennsylvania, 1960), I, 395; and Duncan and Hauser, Housing a Metropolis--Chicago, p. 236.

In their examination of dwellings, households take cost considerations, in either rent or purchase price terms, into account.[1] The upper end of the cost scale is constrained by the household's income.[2] However, instead of analyzing why the household chooses a certain cost level, the relationships between dwelling characteristics and household income will be examined. These relationships provide rough estimates of the criteria households employ.

Evidence that housing expenditures for owners and renters are positively related to income[3] suggests immediately that value of home and rent for a renter occupied unit are positively related to income. That is, the household matches the cost it is willing to pay with a dwelling price. The cost households are willing to pay is a positive function of income. Size and quality of dwelling are also positively associated with income.[4] That is, the more income a household has, the larger the unit and the better the quality the household will buy. Furthermore, the higher the income, the more likely the household will purchase its dwelling.[5]

---

[1]Rossi, Why Families Move, pp. 154ff.; and John B. Lansing and Eva Mueller, Residential Location and Urban Mobility ([Ann Arbor]: Survey Research Center, Institute for Social Research, The University of Michigan, 1964), pp. 20-21. Rossi found that cost considerations become more important when the households finally selected from among a set of alternatives and were less important in the initial selection process. However, the lower importance attached to cost in the initial selection process may not be indicative of the actual importance of cost. Rather, households probably have already in mind the broad cost constraints they must operate under given their income. Therefore when questioned about cost in the initial selection process the households are really responding to the variation in costs within their constraints.

[2]We assume that the level of aspiration of the household in terms of cost factors is realistic in terms of its income.

[3]Maisel and Winnick, "Family Housing Expenditures: Elusive Laws and Intrusive Variances," pp. 371-76.

[4]For size of dwelling see Margaret G. Reid, Housing and Income (Chicago: The University of Chicago Press, 1962), pp. 275-349. Number of rooms was positively related to both measured income and permanent income. For a discussion of permanent income, see Reid, Housing and Income, pp. 8-40. On the positive relationship between housing quality and income see, Editors of the Journal of Housing, "Six Goals for a Program of Low-Income Housing," The Journal of Housing, XX (May, 1963), 259-65, reprinted in William L. C. Wheaton, Grace Milgram, and Margy E. Meyerson, eds., Urban Housing (New York: The Free Press, 1966), pp. 241-45; and Duncan and Hauser, Housing a Metropolis--Chicago, pp. 126-27.

[5]Martin Meyerson, Barbara Terrett, and William L. C. Wheaton, Housing, People, and Cities (New York: McGraw-Hill Book Company, 1962), pp. 56-57; and Maisel and Winnick, "Family Housing Expenditures: Elusive Laws and Intrusive Variances," pp. 394-95.

Neighborhood characteristics. --That the characteristics of the neighborhood are important factors in the household's decision concerning a new dwelling is attested to by several studies.[1] A number of tentative findings concerning the criteria households employ when analyzing their neighborhood are available.[2]

In Peterson's study of perception of neighborhood appearance, the two most important criteria which the respondents seemed to employ in assessing neighborhoods were physical quality (age-expensiveness) and harmony with nature (greenery, open space, nature).[3] In a somewhat similar vein, Lansing and Mueller found that rural settings were preferred by 57 per cent of the people under 35 years and 50 per cent of the couples with children in their sample of residents of metropolitan areas. However, at most 32 per cent of the single people, those over 65 years old, and people with annual incomes under $3000 preferred the rural setting. In addition, the most important favorable comments respondents had toward their neighborhood concerned the kinds of people living there and the physical characteristics such as quietness and cleanliness. Unfavorable comments were directed towards dirtiness, poor upkeep, crowding, undesirable people, too many children, and minority groups.[4]

In summary, people do have preferences with regards to the physical and social characteristics of their neighborhoods. Views toward desirable neighbors seem to indicate a rough preference for living with others of similar socioeconomic status. Preferences in terms of physical characteristics point toward a desire to live in neighborhoods with the highest quality of dwellings and surroundings which the household can afford given their income. Finally, the high preference for rural settings among couples with children, dissatisfaction with number of children in neighborhood, and relatively low per cent of elderly couples preferring a rural setting indicate a life cycle factor in choosing neighborhoods.

---

[1]Rossi, Why Families Move, pp. 154ff.; and Lansing and Mueller, Residential Location and Urban Mobility, pp. 20-21.

[2]Although the criteria refer to attitudes of households toward their own neighborhoods, I believe that they are probably representative of what the household considers when making its residential choice.

[3]George L. Peterson, "A Model of Preference: Quantitative Analysis of the Perception of the Visual Appearance of Residential Neighborhoods," Journal of Regional Science, VII (Summer, 1967), 19-31.

[4]Lansing and Mueller, Residential Location and Urban Mobility, pp. 26-37.

Relative location with respect to the household's movement pattern.--Relative locational considerations are present in the decision about residential location.[1] However, the exact impact of relative location is not entirely clear. As mentioned previously, job location has been found to be relatively unimportant.[2] Perhaps the reason relative location is difficult to isolate is connected to the fact that most moves are relatively short distances. Hence households experience little change in their movement patterns and are therefore not consciously aware of relative locational considerations.

Final decision about moving

After the household has evaluated alternative residential locations a final decision about whether to move or not to move is made. If a residential location meets the aspiration level of the household, presumably the household will relocate. However, if the alternatives do not meet the aspiration level of the household further searching may be decided upon or the household may decide to remain at its original location.[3] If the household decides upon the latter course then we can expect that it will pursue one of the following courses:

1. adjust its need set, or
2. restructure the environment so that it better satisfies the household's needs.[4]

Adjusting the need set would imply either lowering the level of aspiration or increasing the place utility the household derives from its residential location or both. Restructuring the environment could involve such actions as adding rooms to the house, redecorating, and organizing a neighborhood improvement association. The main function of restructuring the environment is to increase the place utility of the household.

Black Residential Choice

There are few specific studies of black residential choice and those which do exist usually focus on Afro-Americans in "integrated" neighborhoods.[5] Therefore in order to

---

[1]Rossi, Why Families Move, pp. 154ff.; and Lansing and Mueller, Residential Location and Urban Mobility, pp. 20-21.

[2]Simmons, "Changing Residence in the City: A Review of Intraurban Mobility," p. 637.

[3]In deciding to continue searching the household may decide to make adjustments in its level of aspiration.

[4]Brown and Moore, "The Intra-Urban Migration Process: A Perspective."

[5]The only exception which I discovered was Lewis G. Watts et al., The Middle-Income Negro Family Faces Urban Renewal (Waltham, Mass.: Brandeis University,

develop some ideas about black residential choice reliance had to be placed on occasional references to it in a diverse literature. As in the previous discussion, black residential choice will be considered in two parts: (1) the decision to seek a new residence and (2) the search for and evaluation of alternative residential locations.

The decision to seek a new residence

As discussed earlier, an increase in the probability of a household deciding to seek a new residence can come from a rise in the level of aspiration or a decline in place utility.[1]

Rise in the level of aspiration.--A study of black families in integrated neighborhoods revealed that the households moved because they wanted to improve their standard of living. In particular these families wanted to own their homes, have more space, and secure better housing.[2] The particular desires probably represent, in part, changing needs with regards to dwellings resulting from increases in income and changes in occupational status.

A rise in the level of aspiration with regards to neighborhoods is evident in the desire for better schools[3] and better areas for raising children.[4]

Decline in place utility.--Changes in life cycle are factors causing Afro-American households to become dissatisfied with their dwelling. Young families are especially likely to want to move.[5] The reasons for such mobility inclinations include marriage and increases in family size.

1964). However, this study is also very limited in that it deals with only a small portion of the Boston black community, the middle-income black family who was in the unusual circumstance of possibly being forced to move.

[1]As discussed earlier, other combinations are also possible. However, these two bring out the major points. The location-utility function of the black household is assumed to be constant.

[2]Henry G. Stetler, Racial Integration in Private Residential Neighborhoods in Connecticut, p. 13.

[3]Ibid.; and Watts et al., The Middle-Income Negro Family Faces Urban Renewal, p. 68.

[4]Watts et al., The Middle-Income Negro Family Faces Urban Renewal, p. 68.

[5]Stetler, Racial Integration in Private Residential Neighborhoods in Connecticut, p. 13; and Watts et al., The Middle-Income Negro Family Faces Urban Renewal, p. 57.

A decline in the place utility a black household derives from its neighborhood is also an important factor in increasing the probability of the household moving.[1] Such dissatisfaction can result from deterioration in the physical condition of the neighborhood or the in-movement of lower classes of residents.

Search for and evaluation of alternative residential locations

Evidence from the Boston study indicates that the middle-income black household will search for a new residential location in relatively close proximity to its present location.[2] Furthermore, Heiges, in a study of intra-urban residential movement in Seattle, 1962-1967, reports that the low income black household moves very short distances.[3] This leads one to suspect that the search was also mainly carried out a short distance from the original residential location.

Although the meager evidence on Afro-American search behavior indicates some correspondence with more general evidence discussed earlier, there is one important difference. Black households are constrained in where they can search by whites.

These constraints are not recent phenomena. For example, detailed studies of two large metropolises, New York and Chicago, demonstrate that hostility and racial antagonism towards Afro-Americans during the period 1890-1920 were instrumental in the development of large confined black living areas which came to be called ghettoes.[4] The Taeubers have provided recent evidence that the segregation of Afro-Americans has remained at a high level from 1940 to 1960 for all regions of the United States.[5] Only a small part of the segregation of Afro-Americans can be attributed to differences in socioeconomic status between the black and white population.[6] Most of the segregation of the

---

[1]E. Franklin Frazier, The Negro Family in Chicago (Chicago: The University of Chicago Press, 1932), pp. 110-12; Stetler, Racial Integration in Private Residential Neighborhoods in Connecticut, p. 13; and Watts et al., The Middle-Income Negro Family Faces Urban Renewal, p. 68.

[2]Watts et al., The Middle-Income Negro Family Faces Urban Renewal, pp. 56-57.

[3]Harvey E. Heiges, "Nere-Migration in Seattle, 1962-1967" (unpublished Ph.D. dissertation, Department of Geography, University of Washington, 1968), pp. 114-15.

[4]Osofsky, Harlem: The Making of a Ghetto; and Spear, Black Chicago: The Making of a Negro Ghetto, 1890-1920. A general discussion of the early development and later growth of the large ghettoes is contained in Weaver, The Negro Ghetto, pp. 8-51 and 99-124.

[5]Taeuber and Taeuber, Negroes in Cities, pp. 28-68.

[6]For example, see J. R. Meyer, J. F. Kain, and M. Wohl, The Urban Transportation Problem (Cambridge, Mass.: Harvard University Press, 1965), pp. 166-67; Taeuber

black population seems to be attributable to constraints operating in the housing market.

The constraints on black housing choice include the personal prejudices and desire of home owners and the institutionalized practices of discrimination of such groups as real estate brokers, salesmen, banks, and housing developers.[1] The constraints imposed by white home owners have ranged from outright terrorist activities to the simple refusal to sell to Afro-Americans. Other constraints have involved real estate agents not making housing listings available, financial institutions making it difficult for black people to get loans to purchase housing, and housing developers excluding Afro-Americans from new suburban housing developments.[2]

Within the limits of these constraints, the expansion in the housing stock available to black households in non-southern cities generally takes place on the periphery of the continuous black residential areas where black households replace white households.[3] In fact this change in occupancy is probably the primary mechanism by which the housing stock available to black households is increased in non-southern cities.[4] In southern cities, on the other hand, black households have greater access to new housing.[5] Nevertheless, black households in southern cities as well as non-southern cities are limited in their choice of residence. Hence most black households are restricted to searching for and evaluating alternative locations within the black housing market.

The criteria black households employ in evaluating alternative residential locations will be considered under the same three headings used in the discussion of general residential choice: dwelling characteristics, neighborhood characteristics, and relative location with respect to the household's movement pattern.

---

and Taeuber, Negroes in Cities, pp. 69-95; and Karl E. Taeuber, "The Effect of Income Redistribution on Racial Residential Segregation," Urban Affairs Quarterly, IV (September, 1968), 10.

[1]Ohio Civil Rights Commission, Discrimination in Housing in Ohio (Columbus, Ohio, 1963).

[2]For example see Glazer and McEntire, eds., Studies in Housing and Minority Groups; Gries and Ford, eds., Negro Housing; Tilly, Jackson, and Kay, Race and Residence in Wilmington, Delaware; and Weaver, The Negro Ghetto.

[3]This occupancy change is especially well-documented for Chicago from 1920 to 1950 in Duncan and Duncan, The Negro Population of Chicago, pp. 87-107. A recent study of Chicago indicates that the pattern of occupancy change has remained essentially the same through 1968. See Brian J. L. Berry et al., "Down from the Summit" (unpublished paper, Center for Urban Studies, University of Chicago, 1969), pp. 4-11.

[4]Chicago is one example. See Berry et al., "Down from the Summit," pp. 112-30.

[5]Taeuber and Taeuber, Negroes in Cities, p. 124.

Dwelling characteristics.--The relationship between the life cycle of the black family and the criteria black households employ in evaluating a dwelling is relatively unexplored. One of the few findings is that there is an increasing tendency to own the home with increasing numbers of children in the family.[1]

However, there is some evidence about the relationship between income or status and dwelling characteristics. For example, in Chicago Frazier found that home ownership was a positive function of social status and income.[2] Frazier also claimed that home ownership was relatively high among the black upper class in southern and border cities.[3]

In addition, income is positively related to the value and rent of dwellings,[4] and the quality of dwellings.[5] Thus, by paying more rent the black household acquires better quality housing.[6]

Neighborhood characteristics.--When deciding upon a neighborhood, the low income black household tends to stay primarily within low income areas.[7] Of course the income constraint is probably of crucial importance for the low income household. In a somewhat similar fashion it has been reported that the black middle class prefers to live near neighbors of roughly similar income and educational background.[8] In terms of spatial patterning the upper classes tend to move toward the periphery of the black community.

---

[1]Duncan and Hauser, Housing a Metropolis--Chicago, p. 249. Two authors have asserted that the "new Negro middle class" has housing preferences similar to whites of the same income levels and family structures. However they do not explicitly state what the relationship is between family type and dwelling characteristics. See Grier and Grier, "Market Characteristics in Interracial Housing," pp. 52-53.

[2]Frazier, The Negro Family in Chicago, pp. 126-36.

[3]E. Franklin Frazier, The Negro in the United States (New York: The Macmillan Company, 1949), pp. 294-95.

[4]Reid, Housing and Income, pp. 389-90. Reid analyzed the relationship between normal income and value and rent of dwellings. She could find no difference between whites and nonwhites in terms of how much housing each group acquires per normal income.

[5]Duncan and Hauser, Housing a Metropolis--Chicago, p. 190.

[6]Ibid., p. 194; and Chester Rapkin, "Price Discrimination Against Negroes in the Rental Housing Market," Essays in Urban Land Economics, Real Estate Research Program (Los Angeles: University of California, 1966), p. 342.

[7]Heiges, "Nere-Migration in Seattle, 1962-1967," p. 124.

[8]Frazier, The Negro in the United States, p. 301; and Grier and Grier, "Market Characteristics in Interracial Housing," p. 53.

Such would seem to be the conclusion of the studies which found an increase in socio-economic status with increasing distance from the city center.[1]

Relative location with respect to the household's movement pattern.--Because of the relatively circumscribed area within which black households must live, they frequently cannot consider residential locations which are in a desirable location with regards to their job location. For example, in a study of the residential distribution of the employees of Argonne National Laboratory, Galt discovered that black employees had to travel farther to work than their white counterparts in every occupation. This occurs because black employees are restricted to living in two large areas in Chicago, the West Side and the South Side. However, the laboratory is located more than 18 miles southwest of the Loop.[2]

Further evidence that black households have difficulty finding a desirable location with respect to their job location is provided in a study of Chicago and Detroit. In both cities most black households must live in a central location. The researchers suggest that centrally employed nonwhites either prefer to spend less on transportation and more on housing or by virtue of housing segregation have to pay more for housing and hence save on transportation compared with centrally employed whites. However, nonwhites employed in the outer rings of the cities live closer to the CBD than similarly employed white workers. Thus nonwhites employed in the outer rings pay both higher transportation costs and higher housing costs than whites employed in the outer rings.[3]

However, in terms of being able to live near their friends and relatives, black households seem to be more successful. I know of no evidence to the contrary. In fact black households seem to prefer to live relatively close to their friends and acquaintances which means, of course, living in black residential areas.[4]

---

[1]Duncan and Duncan, The Negro Population of Chicago, p. 292; Frazier, The Negro Family in Chicago, pp. 86-116; and Leo F. Schnore, "Social Class Segregation among Nonwhites in Metropolitan Centers," Demography, II (1965), 126-33.

[2]John E. Galt, "The Residential Distribution of the Employees of Argonne National Laboratory: Patterns and Implications" (unpublished Master's dissertation, Department of Geography, University of Chicago, 1968).

[3]Meyer, Kain, and Wohl, The Urban Transportation Problem, pp. 156-59. The housing costs were based on a unit and adjusted quality space basis.

[4]As far back as 1899, DuBois found that Afro-Americans prefer to live near their friends. See W. E. B. DuBois, The Philadelphia Negro, Publications of the University of Pennsylvania: Political Economy and Public Law, No. 14 (Philadelphia: The University of Pennsylvania, 1899; reprinted New York: Schocken Books, 1967), pp. 296-97. I drew the same conclusion about the black household's preferences from Watts et al., The Middle-Income Negro Family Faces Urban Renewal. However, the authors tended to downgrade the preference of black households for living near their friends. They explained

In this discussion the role of public housing in the residential choices of black households has been ignored. In cities where standard quality public housing is available to low income black families, one would expect that those black families in public housing would occupy housing of better quality than expected based upon their income. Since public authorities have made the decision concerning the location of the public housing, the low income black family that wishes to live in public housing has little choice concerning neighborhood characteristics and the relative location of the public housing with respect to the household's movement pattern.

---

the lack of mobility and the few residential changes in terms of such things as economic motives and fear of discrimination.

CHAPTER III

STUDY DESIGN: SAMPLE, UNITS OF ANALYSIS, AND VARIABLES

A study of the spatial differentiation of black households in cities can be approached from two distinct standpoints. The first emphasizes the wide range of factors which might contribute to the spatial pattern of black households in a city. These factors would include history of settlement, racial attitudes, economic conditions, etc. Such in-depth study must of necessity most frequently be limited to one city. A second approach emphasizes the search for patterns characteristic of cities in general. The depth of analysis when dealing with a larger sample of cities is of necessity less than in the first approach. Since there are few prior empirical studies of the spatial differentiation of black households in cities but several in-depth investigations, the second approach will be taken. The advantage is in developing generalizations which are not unique to any one city.

Sample of Cities

A prior study of 145 SMSA's using data for 1960 revealed, by using factorial methods of data analysis, that cities varied in seven distinct ways with respect to the characteristics of their nonwhite populations, as indicated in Table 1.[1] Except for factor two, which identified the large concentrations of "other races" in the western United States, the factors generally refer to the Afro-American population since they comprised 91.4 per cent of the nonwhites in the study. Because the variables included in this earlier study using cities as observations were essentially the same type of variables that will be used in the present study of black residential areas within SMSA's in 1960, the factor scores of the 145 SMSA's on the seven factors provide a basis for choosing a sample of SMSA's for the present study. Since factors one and three in Table 1 were the two most important factors, and at the same time corresponded to concepts basic to the present study, they were used as a basis for stratifying SMSA's.

---

[1]David R. Meyer, "Classification of SMSA's Based upon Characteristics of Their Nonwhite Populations," in Classification of Cities: New Methods and Evolving Uses, ed. by Brian J. L. Berry (International City Managers Association and Resources for the Future, forthcoming).

TABLE 1[a]

VARIANCE OF NONWHITE POPULATION ACCOUNTED FOR BY FACTORS

Factor No.	Factor Description	Per Cent of Total Variance	Per Cent of 7-Factor Variance
1	Socioeconomic status	19.6	23.2
2	Variations among nonwhite groups in socioeconomic status levels	16.5	19.4
3	Stage in life cycle	13.3	15.7
4	Size of housing and unemployment	10.7	12.6
5	Housing type	10.3	12.2
6	Position in urban hierarchy	8.5	10.0
7	Service workers	5.9	6.9
	Totals	84.8	100.0

[a]David R. Meyer, "Classification of SMSA's Based upon Characteristics of Their Nonwhite Populations," in Classification of Cities: New Methods and Evolving Uses, ed. by Brian J. L. Berry (International City Managers Association and Resources for the Future, forthcoming), Table 1.

It was decided that the list of SMSA's from which the sample would be chosen should not include SMSA's with fewer than 31 census tracts for which separate data on nonwhites was given. Since some tracts in each city had to be dropped from the study for various reasons, 31 provided a base from which I would be certain of having an adequate number of tracts for statistical analysis. Therefore one limitation of this study is that it does not include SMSA's with relatively small Afro-American populations. With this lower limit of 31 census tracts I ended up with 37 SMSA's with 31 or more census tracts.[1] These 37 SMSA's were then divided into two groups: group one containing 19 cities with more than 50 census tracts and group two containing 18 cities with 31-49 census tracts. The reasons for using two groups was to insure that when the sample was drawn, cities with a wide range of census tracts would be included in the study.

Within each group the SMSA's were ranked according to their factor scores on factor one in Table 1 and then the ranking was split into two equal parts.[2] In each subgroup the cities were ranked according to their factor scores on factor three in Table 1

[1]Honolulu, Hawaii, was excluded even though it contains more than 31 census tracts for nonwhites because most of the nonwhites are not Afro-Americans.

[2]If the group in a ranking contained an odd number of cities the extra city was randomly assigned to one of the two subgroups.

TABLE 2

CITIES IN STUDY

SMSA[a]	Number of Census Tracts Included in Study[b]
Atlanta, Georgia	42
Baltimore, Maryland	65
Birmingham, Alabama	47
Cincinnati, Ohio	24
Columbia, South Carolina	12
Columbus, Ohio	16
Detroit, Michigan	141
Kansas City, Missouri	26
Los Angeles, California	91
Memphis, Tennessee	44
Milwaukee, Wisconsin	18
Philadelphia, Pennsylvania	109
Richmond, Virginia	24
St. Louis, Missouri	44
Shreveport, Louisiana	24
Tampa-St. Petersburg, Florida	21

[a]The SMSA name is identified by the major central city in each SMSA.

[b]U. S., Bureau of the Census, U. S. Censuses of Population and Housing: 1960, Census Tracts (Washington, D. C.: U. S. Government Printing Office, 1962).

TABLE 3

VARIABLES

Variable Name	Description
DISCBD	Distance of center of tract from CBD, in natural logs of miles
FAMINC	Median family income
MDRENT	Median rent of renter occupied units
MROOMS	Median number of rooms
NRL/HD	Ratio of nonrelatives of heads of households to heads of households
OTR/HD	Ratio of other relatives of heads of households to heads of households
PCONOC	Per cent occupied units owner occupied
PCPP18	Per cent population under 18 years old
PCPR39	Per cent occupied units built 1939 or earlier
PCSFDW	Per cent occupied units single family dwellings
PCSOND	Per cent occupied units sound with all plumbing facilities
VALOWN	Median value of owner occupied units
WIV/HD	Per cent households which are husband-wife households

and then each subgroup was divided into two equal parts. Thus four subgroups resulted in both group one and group two. Two SMSA's were randomly chosen from each subgroup. The sixteen SMSA's forming the sample of cities in this study are listed in Table 2 and their locations in the United States are indicated on the Frontispiece map.

Units of Analysis and Variables

As indicated above, the census tracts studied in each of the sixteen SMSA's included all tracts with separate data on nonwhites. By definition of the U. S. Bureau of the Census these tracts have 400 or more nonwhites. In order to assure that the census tracts included in my study actually provide data on Afro-American households and their housing, tracts had to meet all of the following criteria to be included in the analyses.

1. Ninety per cent or more of the nonwhites must be Afro-Americans.
2. The tract must not have more than 10 per cent of its nonwhite population in group quarters.
3. The tract must contain data on all housing variables.[1]

The number of census tracts included in the subsequent analyses for each of the sixteen SMSA's in 1960 is listed in Table 2. The variables for each census tract included in the study are listed in Table 3. In the following discussion I will frequently employ only the six-letter acronym indicated for each variable.

---

[1] This restriction was not of my own choosing. The Census Bureau does not provide housing data for certain variables when there are less than 400 housing units occupied by nonwhites in a census tract. Since several of these variables were crucial to my study I had to discard tracts for which the variables were not shown in the tract listings.

CHAPTER IV

RELATIONS BETWEEN INCOME AND HOUSING

The first step in the investigation demands that the relationship between the spatial variation of black households by income and the spatial variation of housing characteristics among black residential areas be analyzed. In most of the analyses the existence of a given set of housing characteristics which are distributed among black residential areas in some manner will be assumed. The focus will be on whether there is any correspondence between the given spatial differentiation of housing characteristics and the spatial differentiation of black households by income.

Income and Price of Housing

The previous review of residential choice literature indicates that at the individual household level the amount of money spent on housing is positively related to the household's income. Although specific studies are scarce, Margaret Reid's work indicates that the same relationship seems to hold for black households.[1] At the same time housing of similar value and rent is typically constructed in relatively close proximity. This pattern occurs in part because developers prefer to build for a relatively homogeneous market. As evidence of this I refer to the large suburban developments of identically constructed housing and the similar patterns, perhaps at a somewhat smaller scale, within central cities, where several blocks will have identically constructed housing.

Another closely related reason for housing of similar value and rent being constructed in relatively close proximity is that households prefer living near other households of similar or higher income. Such a preference seems to partly underlie the preferences of households concerning desirable characteristics of neighborhoods[2] reviewed in the discussion of residential choice. This preference may be perceived either implicitly or explicitly by the housing developers who then construct housing for a relatively homo-

---

[1]Reid, Housing and Income, pp. 389-90.

[2]I am not differentiating here between different components of socioeconomic status. Rather I am assuming that household comments about status and social groups apply in particular to income groups.

geneous market. In fact when a developer makes a decision about the selling price of his housing he has effectively limited the households who can purchase his housing to those who can afford it. For example, Gans reports that in the new housing development of Levittown, New Jersey, the selling price for housing was $11,500-14,500 and households had to have a weekly income 10 per cent above the monthly carrying charge to obtain a mortgage loan.[1]

The preference for living near other households of similar or higher income seems to apply in particular to the black household. The claim has been made specifically for the black middle class that they prefer to live near neighbors of roughly similar income and education.[2] In addition, indexes of dissimilarity in residential distribution among occupation groups for employed nonwhite males in 1950 and 1960 (computed by the Taeubers for ten cities)[3] reveal, in general, that Afro-Americans are residentially segregated by occupation among residential areas. However, the segregation is probably not as great as found in white residential areas.[4] Although the relationship between occupational status and income is not one-to-one, the suggestion that black households prefer to live near other households of similar or higher income is not unreasonable.

The following explicit assumptions are now made:

1. The price of housing paid by a black household is a positive function of its income.
2. Housing of similar value and rent is constructed in relatively close proximity, which may be a reflection of the fact that
   a. Housing developers build for a homogeneous market.
   b. Households, both black and white, prefer living near other households of similar or higher income.

Based on these assumptions, I hypothesize that

> the median family income (FAMINC) of a black residential area is a positive linear function of the median value of owner occupied units (VALOWN) and median rent of renter occupied units (MDRENT).

This hypothesis is formulated in terms of two simple linear regression models

$$FAMINC = a + b(VALOWN) \quad (8)$$

$$FAMINC = a + b(MDRENT) \quad (9)$$

where a and b are parameters of the model.

---

[1]Herbert J. Gans, The Levittowners (New York: Random House, Inc., 1967), pp. 5-14.

[2]Frazier, The Negro in the United States, p. 301; and Grier and Grier, "Market Characteristics in Interracial Housing," p. 53.

[3]The ten cities were Detroit, Cleveland, Philadelphia, St. Louis, Washington, Baltimore, New Orleans, Atlanta, Birmingham, and Memphis.

[4]Taeuber and Taeuber, Negroes in Cities, pp. 181-82.

Median family income (FAMINC) and median value of owner occupied units (VALOWN)

The results of the analysis of model 8 are contained in Table 4.[1] In twelve of the sixteen cities, the null hypothesis of no linear association between FAMINC and VALOWN is rejected at least at the 0.05 level of significance.[2] Therefore I conclude that there is a significant positive linear association between FAMINC and VALOWN. However, the linear model is not an especially powerful predictor of FAMINC. The r^2 values range from 0.004 to 0.499.

TABLE 4

RELATION OF MEDIAN FAMILY INCOME (FAMINC) TO MEDIAN VALUE OF OWNER OCCUPIED UNITS (VALOWN) AND MEDIAN RENT OF RENTER OCCUPIED UNITS (MDRENT)

City	Independent Variables			
	VALOWN		MDRENT	
	r	r^2	r	r^2
Atlanta	.450[a]	.203	.767[a]	.589
Baltimore	.706[a]	.499	.831[a]	.691
Birmingham	.194	.038	.599[a]	.358
Cincinnati	.611[a]	.373	.917[a]	.841
Columbia	-.064	.004	.600[b]	.360
Columbus	.547[b]	.299	.803[a]	.644
Detroit	.538[a]	.290	.812[a]	.659
Kansas City	.673[a]	.453	.863[a]	.745
Los Angeles	.466[a]	.217	.785[a]	.616
Memphis	.064	.004	.692[a]	.479
Milwaukee	.537[b]	.289	.923[a]	.852
Philadelphia	.637[a]	.406	.816[a]	.665
Richmond	.583[a]	.340	.725[a]	.526
St. Louis	.565[a]	.319	.827[a]	.684
Shreveport	.472[b]	.223	.805[a]	.648
Tampa-St. Petersburg	-.228	.052	.747[a]	.558

[a]Linear model significant at 0.01 level.

[b]Linear model significant at 0.05 level.

[1]Strictly speaking the analysis of the linear model involves a test of the significance of the regression coefficient b. Since in most of my analyses the regression coefficient per se is not of particular interest I will only show the correlation coefficient in these cases. The test of significance which is indicated over the correlation coefficient should be understood to be a test of significance of the regression model.

[2]The probability of obtaining twelve or more significant results out of sixteen at the 0.05 level purely by chance is $p < 0.0005$.

In cities where the income of Afro-American families is very low one may expect that the individual household demand for housing is low. Therefore, because of the low level of demand, there may be relatively small variation in the value of owner occupied dwellings. Hence differentiation of residential areas by VALOWN may be slight. If Atlanta, Birmingham, Columbia, Memphis, Richmond, Shreveport, and Tampa-St. Petersburg are classified as southern cities, then I conclude from data on median family income in Table 5 that black families in southern cities have lower incomes than black families in non-southern cities.[1] Therefore, I hypothesize that the r relating FAMINC and VALOWN tends to be lower in southern cities than in non-southern cities. To test the hypothesis the Kruskal and Wallis[2] elaboration of Wilcoxon's individual comparisons by ranking methods was used.[3] The basic idea in the statistical test is to decide whether or not the samples in question come from the same population, that is, whether or not the mean rank based on r of southern cities is smaller than would be expected if the ranks were selected at random without replacement.[4] The results of the analysis are contained in Table 6.

Although the allocation of cities to the categories South and Non-South is admittedly crude the null hypothesis that the two samples (South and Non-South) come from the same population is rejected with $p < 0.01$ using a 0.01 level of significance. Based on the ranks, the hypothesis that there is a lower relationship between FAMINC and VALOWN in southern cities than in non-southern cities is tentatively accepted.

However, caution must be emphasized in interpreting this result. First, some important errors are inherent in the data. For example, the U. S. Census reports the median value of owner occupied dwellings of a census tract only down to $5000. For those tracts where the median value is below $5000 the value is merely indicated as below $5000. When this occurred the value was recorded as $5000 so the observation could be retained in the analysis. The problem is not serious in cities where the value of black owner occupied dwellings tends to be high. However, in cities where the value is low there will, of course, be more census tracts where VALOWN is below $5000. In Table 7 are indicated the per cent of the census tracts in each city with VALOWN recorded as equal to $5000.

---

[1]Every city classified as southern had a lower median black family income than every non-southern city.

[2]William H. Kruskal and W. Allen Wallis, "Use of Ranks in One-Criterion Variance Analysis," Journal of the American Statistical Association, XLVII (December, 1952), 583-621.

[3]Frank Wilcoxon, "Individual Comparisons by Ranking Methods," Biometrics Bulletin, I (December, 1945), 80-83.

[4]The cities are ranked from one (lowest r) to sixteen (highest r).

TABLE 5

BLACK MEDIAN FAMILY INCOME IN SMSA'S

SMSA	Median Family Income[a]
Atlanta	3033
Baltimore	4130
Birmingham	2944
Cincinnati	3946
Columbia	2267
Columbus	4436
Detroit	4385
Kansas City	4063
Los Angeles	5163
Memphis	2666
Milwaukee	4872
Philadelphia	4291
Richmond	3447
St. Louis	3622
Shreveport	2268
Tampa-St. Petersburg	2976

[a]U. S., Bureau of the Census, U. S. Censuses of Population and Housing: 1960, Census Tracts (Washington, D. C.: U. S. Government Printing Office, 1962), Table P-4. This is the median family income for all black families in the SMSA, not the mean of the median family income for census tracts.

TABLE 6

RANK OF r BY REGION FOR FAMINC VS. VALOWN

South		Non-South	
Rank	City	Rank	City
1	Tampa-St. Petersburg	6	Los Angeles
2	Columbia	8	Milwaukee
3	Memphis	9	Detroit
4	Birmingham	10	Columbus
5	Atlanta	11	St. Louis
7	Shreveport	13	Cincinnati
12	Richmond	14	Philadelphia
		15	Kansas City
		16	Baltimore

$n = 7$ $\bar{R} = 4.857$ uncorrected for continuity

$R = 34$ $\sigma_{\bar{R}}^2 = 3.6375$

Unit normal deviate = -2.70 One-tail test, $P < .01$

TABLE 7

PER CENT TRACTS WITH MEDIAN VALUE OF OWNER OCCUPIED UNITS (VALOWN) ENTERED AS $5000

City	Per Cent VALOWN $5000
Atlanta	7.1
Baltimore	15.4
Birmingham	27.7
Cincinnati	0.0
Columbia	33.3
Columbus	0.0
Detroit	0.0
Kansas City	0.0
Los Angeles	0.0
Memphis	4.5
Milwaukee	0.0
Philadelphia	11.9
Richmond	8.3
St. Louis	13.6
Shreveport	41.7
Tampa-St. Petersburg	9.5

All of the cities classified as South in Table 6 have non-zero percentages. Two cities, Birmingham and Columbia, with r's of .194 and -.064 respectively, have a large proportion of their tracts with a VALOWN of $5000. However, Memphis with an r of .064 has only 4.5 per cent of its tracts with VALOWN of $5000. Thus, although the problem of a lower limit on recorded census tract statistics may contribute to lower r's it is not the only reason.

An additional factor is that even though the Non-South ranks higher on the r's, the values for r's were not very high even within the Non-South category. Perhaps FAMINC and VALOWN are not related much among black residential areas or perhaps other factors are obscuring the relationship.

Median family income (FAMINC) and median rent of renter occupied units (MDRENT)

In model 9

$$FAMINC = a + b(MDRENT)$$

I hypothesize that FAMINC is a linear function of MDRENT. The results of the analysis of model 9 are contained in Table 4. As is clearly evident, the linear model is significant for all of the cities. Therefore, the hypothesis of a positive linear relationship between FAMINC and MDRENT is accepted. Furthermore, since the r^2 for most of the cities is above 0.500, this implies that there is a strong linear relationship between FAMINC and MDRENT among black residential areas in cities.

Using a test of homogeneity of k values of the correlation coefficient r described in Edwards,[1] a chi square of 23.553 with 15 degrees of freedom was obtained which is significant at the 0.05 level. Therefore the correlation coefficients are homogeneous. That is, the degree of linear association between FAMINC and MDRENT among black residential areas in the 16 cities is similar. If the initial assumptions concerning the price paid by black households for housing and the spatial clustering of housing by rent are true, it would appear that black households have spatially segregated themselves in residential areas such that the higher the median rent of the residential area the higher the median family income of the black households who choose to live in the residential area.[2]

Comparison of median value of owner occupied units (VALOWN) and median rent of renter occupied units (MDRENT)

It has been shown that there is a significant linear relationship of FAMINC with VALOWN and MDRENT among black residential areas within most of the sixteen cities.[3]

---

[1]Allen L. Edwards, Experimental Design in Psychological Research (rev. ed.; New York: Holt, Rinehart and Winston, 1960), pp. 83-85.

[2]Of course, I am not saying that rent influences the family income of the individual household.

[3]At this point a comment is in order on the discrepancy between my results for Los Angeles concerning the relationship between income and value and rent of housing among black residential areas and results reported in Leland S. Burns and Alvin J. Harman, The Complex Metropolis, Part 6: Profile of the Los Angeles Metropolis, Its People and Its Homes, Research Report No. 9, Housing, Real Estate, and Urban Land Studies Program (Los Angeles: University of California, 1968), pp. 48-49. Burns and Harman report that the correlation of nonwhite family incomes with housing values and rents was 0.19 and 0.24 respectively among census tracts in Los Angeles in 1960. They conclude that nonwhites do not live in housing appropriate to their income. However, my results, which apply only to Afro-Americans, showed that the correlation of income with value and rent of housing was 0.466 and 0.785 respectively. Therefore, my results suggest that the findings of Burns and Harman do not apply to Afro-Americans. Since Afro-Americans comprised roughly 78 per cent of all nonwhites in the Los Angeles SMSA in 1960, Burns's and Harman's results ought to be applicable at least to Afro-Americans. I believe there are two major components of the data used by Burns and Harman which could contribute to their findings. First, they did not differentiate nonwhites by race. Hence regularities in the relationship between income and housing value and rent present among each nonwhite group may be canceled out when all nonwhite groups are considered as one group. Secondly, from what I can tell from their data, they used nonwhite family income but correlated this with median value and rent of all housing located in a census tract occupied by both whites and nonwhites. I believe better housing variables would have been median value and rent of nonwhite occupied housing. Granted that my results for Los Angeles apply only to census tracts with 400 or more nonwhites of whom 90.0 per cent or more are

However, the strength of the linear relationship of VALOWN and MDRENT with FAMINC is quite different within every city. In most cities the r^2 of MDRENT with FAMINC is substantially larger than the r^2 of VALOWN with FAMINC. What accounts for this difference?

One possible explanation is that the lower r^2 for VALOWN occurs because there is more error in the measurement of value of owner occupied units than in the measurement of rent of renter occupied units. The value of housing is estimated by the owner. His estimate may be based on his original purchase price, the purchase price plus interest, or what he hopes to sell the housing for. These estimates may differ significantly from what an outside observer may estimate to be the value of the owner's house. However, rent is much easier to estimate since the renter usually knows the exact amount of money he pays for rent each month.

Another explanation for the lower r^2 for VALOWN may be the occurrence of elderly retired people in housing whose value does not match their income. Elderly retired people tend to have a relatively low income. However, the housing which they own was probably purchased and paid for when their incomes were higher. Therefore the correlations for VALOWN and FAMINC tend to be low.

Finally, a third explanation for the lower r^2 of VALOWN than MDRENT may be that the value of owner occupied dwellings is less responsive to market demand within a residential area than is rent of renter occupied units. Therefore residential areas tend to have a greater mixture of values of owner occupied units than rents of renter occupied units. Hence the correlation of median family income (FAMINC) with median value of owner occupied units (VALOWN) is lower than the correlation of FAMINC with median rent of renter occupied units (MDRENT).

Income and Owner Occupancy

At the level of individual choice, the suggestion has been made that the higher the income of the household the more likely they will purchase their dwelling.[1] Such a situation may arise because the prevailing view in American society is that ownership is "good." Thus, if capability of owning is a positive function of income because of the large initial

---

Afro-Americans, I believe my results cast considerable doubt on the conclusions of Burns and Harman as these are applicable to Afro-Americans in Los Angeles. This is not to say that the relationship between income and housing value and rent among Afro-Americans is the same as among whites. In fact, this relationship among Afro-Americans may be lower than among whites due especially to discrimination in housing. Nevertheless, income and housing value and rent are related among Afro-Americans in Los Angeles using census tracts as the units of analysis.

[1]Meyerson, Terrett, and Wheaton, Housing, People, and Cities, pp. 56-57.

investment or other reasons, we have the above pattern of ownership being related to income.[1]

From the literature on black households the inference can also be made that the higher the income of the black household the more likely they will purchase their dwelling. For example, Stetler found that the black families, whom I would roughly identify as middle income, left their former neighborhoods because they wanted to own their homes.[2] In his study of Chicago Frazier presented evidence which indicated that home ownership among black families was related to social status and income.[3] Frazier also claimed that home ownership was high among the wealthy members of the black upper class in southern and border cities.[4]

Assuming that ownership is probably strongly related to income among black families and assuming that households prefer to live near other households of similar or higher income, then one could hypothesize that

> the percent of the occupied units which are owner occupied (PCONOC) in a black residential area is positively related to the median family income (FAMINC) of the residential area.

Based on the results reported in Table 8, the null hypothesis of no linear association between PCONOC and FAMINC is rejected for thirteen of the sixteen cities.[5] Therefore I conclude that there is a significant linear association between PCONOC and FAMINC. For eight of the cities the r^2 values in Table 8 are above 0.500, indicating that the linear relationship between FAMINC and PCONOC is fairly strong.

The relationship between income and owner occupancy at the level of the individual household may be lower in southern cities than in non-southern cities due to the fact that housing costs are low in southern cities. The low housing costs may enable even relatively low income families to own their homes. Therefore, I hypothesize that the r's relating PCONOC and FAMINC would be lower in southern cities than in non-southern cities. The Kruskal and Wallis rank test is used to examine this hypothesis.[6] The test is

---

[1] I think it would be difficult to separate tendency to own from income capability of owning.

[2] Stetler, Racial Integration in Private Residential Neighborhoods in Connecticut, pp. 7-14.

[3] Frazier, The Negro Family in Chicago, pp. 126-36.

[4] Frazier, The Negro in the United States, pp. 294-95.

[5] The probability of obtaining thirteen or more significant results out of sixteen at the 0.05 level of significance purely by chance is $p < 0.0005$.

[6] Kruskal and Wallis, "Use of Ranks in One-Criterion Variance Analysis," pp. 583-621.

TABLE 8

RELATION OF PER CENT OWNER OCCUPIED UNITS (PCONOC) TO MEDIAN FAMILY INCOME (FAMINC)

City	r	r^2
Atlanta	.787[a]	.619
Baltimore	.892[a]	.796
Birmingham	.220	.049
Cincinnati	.718[a]	.515
Columbia	.383	.147
Columbus	.596[b]	.355
Detroit	.737[a]	.544
Kansas City	.899[a]	.808
Los Angeles	.718[a]	.516
Memphis	.592[a]	.351
Milwaukee	.874[a]	.764
Philadelphia	.871[a]	.758
Richmond	.683[a]	.467
St. Louis	.572[a]	.327
Shreveport	.404	.163
Tampa-St. Petersburg	.680[a]	.462

[a]Correlation coefficient significant at 0.01 level.

[b]Correlation coefficient significant at 0.05 level.

whether or not the mean rank based on r of southern cities is smaller than would be expected if the ranks were selected at random without replacement. Based on the results in Table 9 the null hypothesis that the two samples (South and Non-South) come from the same population is rejected with $p < 0.02$ using a 0.05 level of significance. Thus, the hypothesis that there is a lower relationship between PCONOC and FAMINC among black residential areas in southern cities than in non-southern cities is tentatively accepted. One interesting exception to this pattern is that the r for Atlanta is higher than five cities in the Non-South category.

However, the variation in per cent owner occupied dwellings (PCONOC) among residential areas is probably not just related to the variation in median family income (FAMINC). Certain types of housing, especially single family dwellings, are more suitable for owner occupancy than are dwellings such as apartment buildings. Hence the spatial distribution of PCONOC is probably highly correlated with the spatial distribution of single family dwelling units. In fact Table 10 does demonstrate that PCONOC is highly correlated with per cent single family dwellings (PCSFDW). The correlations are significant at the 0.05 level in fifteen of the sixteen cities. Ten of the r's are above 0.700.

Nevertheless, though PCSFDW is highly correlated with PCONOC, the earlier discussion of the important tie between owner occupancy and income leads me to hypothesize

TABLE 9

RANK OF r BY REGION FOR PCONOC VS. FAMINC

South		Non-South	
Rank	City	Rank	City
1	Birmingham	4	St. Louis
2	Columbia	6	Columbus
3	Shreveport	9	Cincinnati
5	Memphis	10	Los Angeles
7	Tampa-St. Petersburg	11	Detroit
8	Richmond	13	Philadelphia
12	Atlanta	14	Milwaukee
		15	Baltimore
		16	Kansas City

n = 7

R = 38

$\bar{R}$ = 5.42857 uncorrected for continuity

$\sigma_{\bar{R}}^2 = 1.8214$

Unit normal deviate = -2.28 One-tail test, $p < .02$

TABLE 10

CORRELATION BETWEEN PER CENT OWNER OCCUPIED UNITS (PCONOC) AND PER CENT SINGLE FAMILY DWELLINGS (PCSFDW)

City	r
Atlanta	.804[a]
Baltimore	.428[a]
Birmingham	.571[a]
Cincinnati	.789[a]
Columbia	.716[a]
Columbus	.832[a]
Detroit	.841[a]
Kansas City	.879[a]
Los Angeles	.658[a]
Memphis	.732[a]
Milwaukee	.354
Philadelphia	.696[a]
Richmond	.709[a]
St. Louis	.744[a]
Shreveport	.434[b]
Tampa-St. Petersburg	.799[a]

[a]Correlation coefficient significant at 0.01 level.

[b]Correlation coefficient significant at 0.05 level.

that PCONOC and FAMINC are still highly related, even holding PCSFDW constant. To test this hypothesis the following linear model is proposed:

$$PCONOC = a + b(FAMINC) + c(PCSFDW) \quad (10)$$

The results of the analysis of model 10 are contained in Table 11.

As is evident from Table 11, the partial correlation of FAMINC with PCONOC is relatively unchanged in most of the cities even when PCSFDW is held constant. In thirteen of the sixteen cities the partial correlation of FAMINC with PCONOC is significant. In only one city, Tampa-St. Petersburg, did a previously significant correlation between PCONOC and FAMINC become non-significant when PCSFDW was held constant while in Shreveport the non-significant correlation between PCONOC and FAMINC became significant when PCSFDW was held constant. In two cities, Birmingham and Columbia, the correlation between PCONOC and FAMINC remained non-significant.

Therefore, among black residential areas per cent owner occupied dwellings (PCONOC) is highly related to median family income (FAMINC) regardless of the variation in per cent single family dwellings (PCSFDW). The findings for the sixteen cities seem to support Frazier's contention that home ownership is an important differentiating characteristic of black residential areas in both southern and non-southern cities.[1] The one qualification is that the pattern does not hold in all southern cities. Three of the seven southern cities in the sample, Birmingham, Columbia, and Tampa-St. Petersburg, had non-significant partial correlations of PCONOC and FAMINC. Nevertheless black households seem to segregate themselves among residential areas by income. Since owner occupancy is so highly related to income, the result is a corresponding differentiation of black residential areas by owner occupancy.

Income and Quality of Housing

Evidence on the preferences of Afro-Americans for quality of housing is meager. The Duncan and Hauser study of Chicago is one of the few analyses which demonstrates that there is a rough correlation between income and quality of housing among nonwhites (mainly Afro-Americans).[2] In spite of the meager evidence concerning preferences for quality of housing among Afro-Americans in particular and the population in general, a reasonable assumption is that all households prefer good quality housing. However, those with more money can purchase better quality housing. Therefore, it is assumed that quality of housing is positively associated with income among Afro-American households.

---

[1]Frazier, The Negro Family in Chicago, pp. 126-36; and Frazier, The Negro in the United States, pp. 294-95.

[2]Duncan and Hauser, Housing a Metropolis--Chicago, p. 190.

TABLE 11

SIMPLE CORRELATION OF PER CENT OWNER OCCUPIED UNITS (PCONOC) WITH MEDIAN FAMILY INCOME (FAMINC) AND PARTIAL CORRELATIONS OF PCONOC WITH FAMINC AND PER CENT SINGLE FAMILY DWELLINGS (PCSFDW)

City	Independent Variables[c]		R^2
	FAMINC	PCSFDW	
Atlanta	.787[a]		.619
	.661[a]	.690[a]	.801
Baltimore	.892[a]		.796
	.896[a]	.456[a]	.839
Birmingham	.220		.049
	.179	.560[a]	.347
Cincinnati	.718[a]		.515
	.638[a]	.734[a]	.776
Columbia	.383		.147
	.332	.701[b]	.567
Columbus	.596[b]		.355
	.725[a]	.880[a]	.854
Detroit	.737[a]		.544
	.757[a]	.852[a]	.875
Kansas City	.899[a]		.808
	.740[a]	.679[a]	.897
Los Angeles	.718[a]		.516
	.684[a]	.614[a]	.698
Memphis	.592[a]		.351
	.660[a]	.772[a]	.738
Milwaukee	.874[a]		.764
	.856[a]	.108	.767
Philadelphia	.871[a]		.758
	.820[a]	.548[a]	.831
Richmond	.683[a]		.467
	.693[a]	.718[a]	.742
St. Louis	.572[a]		.327
	.790[a]	.866[a]	.832
Shreveport	.404		.163
	.572[a]	.590[a]	.454
Tampa-St. Petersburg	.680[a]		.462
	.432	.673[a]	.706

[a] Significant at 0.01 level. [b] Significant at 0.05 level.

[c] Partial correlations are on second line for each city.

Yet studies of Afro-Americans in cities leave the impression that black residential areas are relatively undifferentiated by housing quality.[1] In his study of Harlem, Osofsky leaves the impression, perhaps unintentional, that the whole area became a slum during the 1920's.[2] However, the generalizations of Osofsky, Drake and Cayton, and others are influenced not only by the time in which they were written or written about, but also by the emphases of the authors. And in studies of black residential areas the emphases seem to be on the poor quality of housing. Yet in ten of the sixteen cities in this study 50 per cent or more of the Afro-American housing is sound.[3] See Table 12. Such figures do not indicate that all Afro-American housing is poor quality.

Assume that households prefer living near other households of similar or higher income and that builders perceive this preference of households. Furthermore, assume that builders prefer to build housing of similar quality in close proximity since they can then incur savings in the cost of construction by using the same plans and materials for all housing in a particular locale.

Collecting the above assumptions, assume that

1. The quality of housing purchased by a black household is positively related to its income.
2. Housing of similar quality exists in relatively close proximity.

I hypothesize that

> the median family income (FAMINC) of a black residential area is a positive linear function of the per cent of the occupied units which are of sound quality (PCSOND).

This hypothesis can be expressed in the form of a simple linear model.

$$FAMINC = a + b(PCSOND) \qquad (11)$$

The results of the analysis of model 11 are recorded in Table 13.

The linear model is a significant predictor of FAMINC in fourteen of the sixteen cities using a 0.05 level of significance. Therefore the hypothesis that there is a positive linear relation between FAMINC and PCSOND among black residential areas in cities is accepted. That is, the differentiation of black residential areas by quality is matched by

---

[1] For example see St. Clair Drake and Horace R. Cayton, Black Metropolis (2 vols., rev. ed.; New York: Harper & Row, Harper Torchbooks, 1962), II, 658-60. The fact that much of the research for this book on Chicago was done during the Depression of the 1930's may explain the findings. Afro-Americans suffered severely during this period and retrenchment in terms of housing conditions was necessary.

[2] Osofsky, Harlem: The Making of a Ghetto, pp. 127-49.

[3] The criteria sound applies only to housing classified as sound with all plumbing facilities in the 1960 census. Sound does not include housing classified as sound but lacking some or all plumbing facilities in the census. Thus my definition is more restrictive than the definition in the U. S. Census.

TABLE 12

TOTAL PER CENT SOUND HOUSING

City	Total[a] Per Cent Sound
Atlanta	50.2
Baltimore	65.0
Birmingham	33.1
Cincinnati	51.6
Columbia	31.8
Columbus	50.2
Detroit	70.2
Kansas City	57.2
Los Angeles	81.0
Memphis	49.5
Milwaukee	55.0
Philadelphia	66.3
Richmond	51.0
St. Louis	46.1
Shreveport	24.4
Tampa-St. Petersburg	39.5

[a]The total per cent sound is computed on the basis of all tracts with 400 or more non-whites in each city in which Afro-Americans comprise 90 per cent or more of the non-whites. The classification refers to only those sound units with all plumbing facilities. Data are contained in U. S., Bureau of the Census, U. S. Censuses of Population and Housing: 1960, Census Tracts (Washington, D. C.: U. S. Government Printing Office, 1962), Table H-3.

a corresponding differentiation of black households by income. However, the r^2 values for the model are not especially high, indicating that PCSOND by itself does not predict much of the variation in FAMINC. One reason for the low relationship between FAMINC and PCSOND may be that elderly couples who have low incomes can live in housing which is better than expected because the housing was purchased when their incomes were higher. Another reason may be that money available for housing is partly dependent upon size of families. Large families who may have moderately high incomes can actually have less money to spend on housing than small families with lower incomes.

Since income is most likely strongly related to quality of housing at the individual household level, I hypothesize that lower total proportions of sound housing would be found in southern cities than in non-southern cities. To test the hypothesis the Kruskal and Wallis rank test is employed.[1] The test is whether or not the mean rank of total per cent

[1]Kruskal and Wallis, "Use of Ranks in One-Criterion Variance Analysis," pp. 583-621.

TABLE 13

RELATION BETWEEN MEDIAN FAMILY INCOME (FAMINC)
AND PER CENT SOUND UNITS (PCSOND)

City	r	r^2
Atlanta	.548[a]	.301
Baltimore	.682[a]	.465
Birmingham	.654[a]	.428
Cincinnati	.436[b]	.191
Columbia	.540	.292
Columbus	.582[b]	.338
Detroit	.695[a]	.483
Kansas City	.783[a]	.614
Los Angeles	.475[a]	.226
Memphis	.588[a]	.346
Milwaukee	.468[b]	.219
Philadelphia	.709[a]	.503
Richmond	.565[a]	.320
St. Louis	.779[a]	.607
Shreveport	.776[a]	.601
Tampa-St. Petersburg	-.107	.011

[a]Linear model significant at 0.01 level.

[b]Linear model significant at 0.05 level.

sound housing of southern cities (Table 12) is lower than would be expected if the ranks were selected at random without replacement. Based on the results in Table 14 the null hypothesis that the two samples, South and Non-South, come from the same population is rejected. The hypothesis that lower total proportions of sound housing are found in southern cities than in non-southern cities is tentatively accepted.

However, such a finding does not necessarily imply that the relation between median family income (FAMINC) and per cent sound housing (PCSOND) among black residential areas follows the same pattern. In Table 15 a test is reported of whether or not the mean rank based on the correlation between FAMINC and PCSOND in southern cities is lower than would be expected if the ranks were selected at random without replacement. With a $p < .23$ for a one-tailed test, the null hypothesis that the two samples, South and Non-South, come from the same population cannot be rejected. Hence, in spite of the difference between South and Non-South in total per cent sound housing, the two crude regional divisions are not distinguished by differences in correlations between FAMINC and PCSOND within cities. Even southern cities which have low proportions of sound housing may have relatively high correlations between FAMINC and PCSOND among the black residential areas.

TABLE 14

RANK OF TOTAL PER CENT SOUND HOUSING BY REGION

South		Non-South	
Rank	City	Rank	City
1	Shreveport	5	St. Louis
2	Columbia	7.5	Columbus
3	Birmingham	10	Cincinnati
4	Tampa-St. Petersburg	11	Milwaukee
6	Memphis	12	Kansas City
7.5	Atlanta	13	Baltimore
9	Richmond	14	Philadelphia
		15	Detroit
		16	Los Angeles

n = 7
R = 32.5

$\overline{R}$ = 4.643 uncorrected for continuity

$\sigma_{\overline{R}}^2$ = 1.8188

Unit normal deviate = -2.86 One-tail test, $p < .01$

TABLE 15

RANK OF r BY REGION FOR FAMINC VS. PCSOND

South		Non-South	
Rank	City	Rank	City
1	Tampa-St. Petersburg	2	Cincinnati
5	Columbia	3	Milwaukee
6	Atlanta	4	Los Angeles
7	Richmond	8	Columbus
9	Memphis	11	Baltimore
10	Birmingham	12	Detroit
14	Shreveport	13	Philadelphia
		15	St. Louis
		16	Kansas City

n = 7
$\underline{R}$ = 52
$\overline{R}$ = 7.429 uncorrected for continuity

$\overline{R}$ = 7.500 corrected for continuity
$\sigma_{\overline{R}}^2$ = 1.8214

Unit normal deviate = .74 One-tail test, $p < .23$

So far only the relationship between median family income (FAMINC) and per cent sound housing (PCSOND) has been examined. In an earlier discussion it was suggested that those households with more money can purchase better quality housing. However, the factors of value and rent of dwelling which would seem to be intimately related to the quality of the dwelling have been ignored. Part of the price of housing is composed of the cost of constructing and/or maintaining the housing at a particular level of quality. Hence I hypothesize that the variation in quality of dwellings among residential areas is correlated with the variation in value and rent of dwellings. The correlation coefficients are contained in Table 16. The correlation of PCSOND with median value of owner occupied units (VALOWN) is significant at the 0.05 level in fifteen of the sixteen cities and the correlation of PCSOND with median rent of renter occupied units (MDRENT) is significant at the 0.05 level in twelve of the sixteen cities. Therefore variation in quality of dwellings among black residential areas in cities is related to the variation in value and rent of dwellings.

TABLE 16

CORRELATION OF PER CENT SOUND UNITS (PCSOND) WITH MEDIAN VALUE OF OWNER OCCUPIED UNITS (VALOWN) AND MEDIAN RENT OF RENTER OCCUPIED UNITS (MDRENT)

City	VALOWN	MDRENT
Atlanta	.374[a]	.495[a]
Baltimore	.497[a]	.578[a]
Birmingham	.374[a]	.619[a]
Cincinnati	.580[a]	.629[a]
Columbia	.061	.719[a]
Columbus	.639[a]	.310
Detroit	.509[a]	.592[a]
Kansas City	.719[a]	.810[a]
Los Angeles	.401[a]	.489[a]
Memphis	.309[b]	.627[a]
Milwaukee	.517[b]	.366
Philadelphia	.448[a]	.538[a]
Richmond	.735[a]	.214
St. Louis	.631[a]	.849[a]
Shreveport	.711[a]	.753[a]
Tampa-St. Petersburg	.499[b]	.246

[a]Correlation coefficient significant at 0.01 level.

[b]Correlation coefficient significant at 0.05 level.

In the first part of this chapter it was suggested that the value or rent of dwelling purchased by a black household was a function of its income. In turn value and rent are intimately related to the quality of a dwelling. Thus it would seem reasonable to suggest that the relationship between household income and quality of dwelling would cease to exist if value or rent of dwelling was held constant. Assuming regularities in the spatial pattern of housing by value, rent, and quality, I hypothesize that the relationship between FAMINC and PCSOND among black residential areas in a city is non-significant when VALOWN and MDRENT are held constant. To test this hypothesis the following multiple regression model is formulated:

$$\text{FAMINC} = a + b(\text{PCSOND}) + c(\text{VALOWN}) + d(\text{MDRENT}) \tag{12}$$

The results of the analysis are contained in Table 17.

The general tendency was for the partial correlation of per cent sound quality housing (PCSOND) with median family income (FAMINC), holding median value of owner occupied units (VALOWN) and median rent of renter occupied units (MDRENT) constant, to be substantially lower than the simple correlation. Only six of the partial correlations of PCSOND with FAMINC are significantly positive at the 0.05 level, whereas fourteen of the simple correlations between FAMINC and PCSOND are significant. Hence there is some support for not rejecting the hypothesis which states in effect that the relationship between FAMINC and PCSOND can be accounted for by the relationship of FAMINC with VALOWN and MDRENT. Yet the fact cannot be ignored that in six cities the partial correlation of PCSOND with FAMINC was significant. Two possible explanations of this finding are

1. Errors in measurement which obscure the relationship between PCSOND and VALOWN and MDRENT.
2. A strong preference for good quality housing and the maintenance of it which is a function of income but which does not show up in the value or rent of housing.

I do not have any sound explanation for the switch from a significant positive simple correlation between FAMINC and PCSOND in Cincinnati to a significant negative partial correlation of PCSOND with FAMINC. My only guess is that perhaps the occurrence of public housing is affecting the results. Assuming that public housing is generally of good quality and there is an upper limit on the income of households in public housing, then we could observe a pattern where at the same rent higher income households live in housing which is of poorer quality than lower income households. If the public housing is spatially concentrated, then the same pattern might hold for characteristics of residential areas.

Although the relationship between FAMINC and PCSOND is partly accounted for by the association of FAMINC with VALOWN and MDRENT, the discovery of a significant linear relation of FAMINC as a function of PCSOND is still important. Black households are segregated among residential areas by income, corresponding to the variation in quality

TABLE 17

SIMPLE CORRELATION BETWEEN MEDIAN FAMILY INCOME (FAMINC) AND PER CENT SOUND UNITS (PCSOND) AND PARTIAL CORRELATIONS OF FAMINC WITH PCSOND, MEDIAN VALUE OF OWNER OCCUPIED UNITS (VALOWN), AND MEDIAN RENT OF RENTER OCCUPIED UNITS (MDRENT)

City	Independent Variables[c]			R^2
	PCSOND	VALOWN	MDRENT	
Atlanta	.548[a]			.301
	.283	.104	.642[a]	.630
Baltimore	.682[a]			.465
	.345[a]	.568[a]	.727[a]	.832
Birmingham	.654[a]			.428
	.468[a]	-.294[b]	.423[a]	.533
Cincinnati	.436[b]			.191
	-.435[b]	-.036	.892[a]	.873
Columbia	.540			.292
	-.045	-.469	.559	.520
Columbus	.582[b]			.338
	.557[b]	-.133	.790[a]	.771
Detroit	.695[a]			.483
	.362[a]	.281[a]	.687[a]	.751
Kansas City	.783[a]			.614
	.115	.296	.639[a]	.786
Los Angeles	.475[a]			.226
	.060	.354[a]	.723[a]	.673
Memphis	.588[a]			.346
	.283	-.077	.500[a]	.521
Milwaukee	.468[b]			.219
	.309	.074	.898[a]	.872
Philadelphia	.709[a]			.503
	.518[a]	.367[a]	.676[a]	.799
Richmond	.565[a]			.320
	.349	.239	.739[a]	.719
St. Louis	.779[a]			.607
	.259	-.142	.498[a]	.711
Shreveport	.776[a]			.601
	.535[b]	-.359	.596[a]	.751
Tampa-St. Petersburg	-.107			.011
	-.211	-.588[a]	.870[a]	.769

[a]Significant at 0.01 level. [b]Significant at 0.05 level.

[c]Partial correlations are on second line for each city.

of dwellings. Thus statements that all black residential areas are a "slum" cannot be supported by my evidence.

Income and Age of Dwelling

Although there is little specific evidence in the residential choice literature concerning the preferences of households for new housing,[1] there are two interrelated reasons for postulating that the age of the dwelling which the household occupies is positively related to household income. First, new housing is preferable to old housing because new housing contains the latest conveniences and is less likely to be deteriorated. Secondly, new housing costs more than old housing because of rising costs in construction for new housing coupled with lower value of old housing through depreciation. Hence higher income households can afford the new housing while lower income households can only afford the older depreciated housing.

Furthermore, it is assumed that housing is spatially concentrated by age. This occurs partly as a result of mass building of housing in one locale by housing developers. In addition, since vacant land is most prevalent and cheapest on the periphery of cities, new housing tends to be constructed there. Hence older housing is located near the center of cities and new housing on the periphery.

Assuming specifically that age of dwelling is positively related to household income among black households and housing is spatially concentrated by age among black residential areas, I hypothesize that

> the median family income (FAMINC) of a black residential area is a negative function of the percentage of occupied units built before 1939 (PCPR39).

The hypothesis can be expressed in the form of a simple linear model

$$\text{FAMINC} = a - b(\text{PCPR39}) \qquad (13)$$

However, the hypothesis presupposes that housing of a preferred age is actually available to black households. In non-southern cities Afro-Americans are often concentrated relatively close to the central business district (CBD). In the large cities, the origin of the spatial pattern of Afro-Americans probably dates from the large influx of poor black migrants from the South after 1915. These migrants tended to settle in the run-down housing of the cities.[2] Such housing probably was located relatively close to the CBD. The response of whites to the large influx of black residents was the enforcement

---

[1]The one exception is a study by Peterson in which he found a preference for new neighborhoods. See Peterson, "A Model of Preference: Quantitative Analysis of the Perception of the Visual Appearance of Residential Neighborhoods," pp. 19-31.

[2]Weaver, The Negro Ghetto, pp. 25-29.

of strict residential segregation.[1] Thereafter, additions to the black housing stock derived mainly from peripheral expansion of black residential areas outward from the central portions of cities. Hence new housing on the periphery of large non-southern cities is closed to black households. In smaller non-southern cities the first settlement of black households was also probably near the CBD. Constraints on black housing choice probably led to similar spatial patterns of settlement.

However, in southern cities, black households have greater access to new housing.[2] Several factors may explain this condition. One suggestion is that southern cities have more vacant land which can be occupied by black households than do non-southern cities.[3] Secondly, although segregated from whites, clusters of black households in southern cities are relatively scattered about the cities. These scattered clusters partly result from the incorporation of rural black settlements into the cities as they expand.[4] The larger clusters tend to occur in newer southern cities while older southern cities have a wider scattering of black households.[5] Hence, a wide range of housing according to age exists in the black housing market in southern cities. Finally, black households can have access to new housing on the periphery of southern cities. Black settlements on the periphery may evolve from rural black settlements which become incorporated into the city as the city grows. New housing for black households could be built on vacant land in and near these settlements.[6]

Given the above differences between southern and non-southern cities in the spatial pattern of black households, black households in non-southern cities would tend to be concentrated relatively closer to the CBD than in southern cities. An examination of the mean distance of black residential areas from the CBD (mean DISCBD) in Table 18 does not reveal substantial differences between southern and non-southern cities. However, when mean DISCBD is weighted by the total SMSA population, the distance index shows a clear pattern. All distance indexes for southern cities are greater than all distance

---

[1] Ibid., pp. 29-32.

[2] Taeuber and Taeuber, Negroes in Cities, p. 124.

[3] Ibid., p. 125; and Woofter, Negro Problems in Cities, p. 39.

[4] Taeuber and Taeuber, Negroes in Cities, p. 56.

[5] Frazier, The Negro in the United States, p. 237; and Woofter, Negro Problems in Cities, p. 38.

[6] The peripheral settlement of black households may also date from the movement of slaves and free-blacks to the periphery of southern cities in the 1840's and 1850's to escape from white surveillance. See Richard C. Wade, Slavery in the Cities: The South 1820-1860 (London: Oxford University Press, 1964), pp. 275-77.

TABLE 18

DISTANCE OF BLACK RESIDENTIAL AREAS FROM CBD

City	Mean DISCBD[a]	Distance Index[b]
Atlanta	1.308	1.29
Baltimore	1.216	.75
Birmingham	1.591	2.51
Cincinnati	1.265	1.18
Columbia	1.367	5.23
Columbus	.602	.88
Detroit	1.656	.44
Kansas City	1.071	1.03
Los Angeles	2.002	.30
Memphis	1.435	2.29
Milwaukee	.946	.79
Philadelphia	1.331	.31
Richmond	1.001	2.45
St. Louis	1.496	.72
Shreveport	1.720	6.11
Tampa-St. Petersburg	1.165	1.51

[a]DISCBD is expressed in natural logarithms of miles.

[b]Distance Index = $\frac{\text{Mean DISCBD}}{\text{Total SMSA Population}} \times 10^6$.

indexes for non-southern cities. What this means is that, controlling for SMSA population size, Afro-American residential areas tend to be found at greater distances from the CBD in southern cities than in non-southern cities. Assuming that new housing tends to be constructed on the periphery of cities rather than near the CBD, then black families in southern cities would occupy higher proportions of new housing than black families in non-southern cities. The data in Table 19 indicate that of the sixteen cities included in this study, non-southern cities have higher total per cent nonwhite housing built before 1939 than southern cities. In fact, the percentages are so high that model 13 could not legitimately be tested for most of the cities in the non-southern category. The results of the analysis of model 13 are contained in Table 20. The model is significant for only three of the seven cities for which the model is appropriate. Atlanta is the only city for which the r^2 is high enough to merit serious consideration.

Thus, the hypothesis is not supported by the data. Several possible explanations can be offered. First, intervening variables may be obscuring the relation between median family income (FAMINC) and per cent occupied units built pre-1939 (PCPR39). Secondly, black households may not choose new housing in proportion to their income. Thirdly, since black households are confined by various restrictions to older housing in

TABLE 19

TOTAL PER CENT NONWHITE HOUSING BUILT PRE-1939[a]

City	Total Per Cent Pre-1939
Atlanta	57.2
Baltimore	80.0
Birmingham	66.7
Cincinnati	86.4
Columbia	52.4
Columbus	77.6
Detroit	86.1
Kansas City	90.1
Los Angeles	62.4
Memphis	58.5
Milwaukee	92.3
Philadelphia	90.8
Richmond	78.1
St. Louis	84.5
Shreveport	52.2
Tampa-St. Petersburg	57.5

[a]Based on summary statistics contained in U. S., Bureau of the Census, U. S. Censuses of Population and Housing: 1960, Census Tracts (Washington, D. C.: U. S. Government Printing Office, 1962), Table H-3.

central cities they do not have the opportunity to express their preference for new housing. Hence black residential areas are undifferentiated by age of housing. Fourthly, public housing occupied by low income black households is probably new housing. Consequently some low income households as well as high income households occupy new housing. This situation would lower the correlation between FAMINC and PCPR39. Finally, the classification PCPR39 is not a sensitive indicator of variation in old housing since it does not differentiate housing built before 1939.

The anomaly of Atlanta deserves special attention because the model fits the hypothesis and the correlation coefficient is relatively high as compared with the other cities for which the model was computed. For the sake of argument assume that the rationale of the relationship between FAMINC and PCPR39 is essentially correct provided that new housing is available to black households. Therefore, the reason for the model being applicable to Atlanta is probably related to the reasons for the relatively high per cent black housing built since 1939 in Atlanta. A study of housing conditions among Afro-Americans in Atlanta suggests that the black political and business leaders in that city have been instrumental in opening up new housing for black households. In particular, black financial agencies have provided the assets and financing expertise for assisting black house-

TABLE 20

RELATION BETWEEN MEDIAN FAMILY INCOME (FAMINC) AND PER CENT OCCUPIED UNITS BUILT 1939 OR EARLIER (PCPR39)

City	r	r^2
Atlanta	-.617[a]	.380
Baltimore	c	
Birmingham	-.097	.009
Cincinnati	c	
Columbia	-.427	.182
Columbus	c	
Detroit	c	
Kansas City	c	
Los Angeles	-.381[a]	.145
Memphis	-.329[b]	.108
Milwaukee	c	
Philadelphia	c	
Richmond	c	
St. Louis	c	
Shreveport	-.271	.074
Tampa-St. Petersburg	.104	.011

[a]Linear model significant at 0.01 level.

[b]Linear model significant at 0.05 level.

[c]The high total per cent nonwhite housing built before 1939 and the statistics on skew and kurtosis for PCPR39 indicate that the linear relationship would be spurious.

holds. Their role in opening up new housing for black households has been augmented by black brokers, developers, and contractors. The new housing acquired by black households has been in the form of housing developments rather than isolated housing.[1] Since housing of similar age was constructed in relatively close proximity in Atlanta, the end result is a differentiation of black residential areas such that the newer the housing the higher the income of the black households in the residential area.

Income and Distance from City Center

The observation has been made by several scholars, notably Frazier, the Duncans, and Schnore, that the socioeconomic status of Afro-Americans increases with increasing

[1]Robert A. Thompson, Hylan Lewis, and Davis McEntire, "Atlanta and Birmingham: A Comparative Study in Negro Housing," in Studies in Housing and Minority Groups, ed. by Nathan Glazer and Davis McEntire (Berkeley and Los Angeles: University of California Press, 1960), pp. 14-51.

distance from the center of a city.[1] For my purposes I will consider the central business district (CBD) the city center. The reasons given for a spatial pattern where socioeconomic status is positively related to distance from the CBD are based mainly on Burgess' ideas.[2] He seems to argue that a series of concentric zones develop as the city grows. Each zone contains a particular activity with business and manufacturing near the CBD and residential areas toward the periphery. Each zone tends to grow outward. A positive relationship between socioeconomic status and distance from the CBD is implied in Burgess' characterization of the second zone as the area of deterioration, the third zone as containing those who have escaped from the second zone, and the fourth zone as the area of exclusive residential areas.

Burgess' ideas were taken by Frazier and applied to the Afro-American population in Chicago in 1920. Frazier claimed that Afro-Americans first acquired a foothold in the areas of deteriorated housing where rents were cheap around the CBD. From this location the black population expanded in a manner similar to other racial and immigrant groups. The movement was given initial impetus by the expansion of the CBD. Increases in numbers of poor black migrants to Chicago sustained the expansion of the area of black settlement. Poorer people moved into the better residential areas and the residents of these areas moved farther south. Through a process of selection various elements of the black population became segregated in different zones. Implicit in Frazier's arguments was that the black population expanded southward in Chicago in a continual search for better housing.[3]

However, Frazier's formulation and the later analyses of the Duncans and Schnore[4] leave many questions unanswered about why black households locate where they do with regards to the CBD. For example, why is better housing located farther from the CBD than poorer housing? Is a succession process necessary to produce a particular spatial pattern?

According to Alonso, the assumption of a growing city is not necessary in order to have higher income families living farther out from the CBD than lower income

---

[1]Frazier, The Negro Family in Chicago, pp. 86-146; Duncan and Duncan, The Negro Population of Chicago, p. 292; and Schnore, "Social Class Segregation among Nonwhites in Metropolitan Centers," pp. 126-33.

[2]The main outline of Burgess' ideas is found in Ernest W. Burgess, "The Growth of the City: An Introduction to a Research Project," in The City, ed. by Robert E. Park, Ernest W. Burgess, and R. D. McKenzie (Chicago: University of Chicago Press, 1925).

[3]Frazier, The Negro Family in Chicago, pp. 91ff.

[4]Duncan and Duncan, The Negro Population of Chicago; and Schnore, "Social Class Segregation among Nonwhites in Metropolitan Centers."

families.[1] He demonstrates that those households with steeper bid price curves[2] will locate closer to the CBD.[3] Alonso tries to show that families with higher incomes have more gently sloped bid price curves. Therefore if both conditions of the bid price curves hold, Alonso claims that higher income households will tend to live on the periphery of the city and lower income households in central locations. Another way of viewing this phenomenon is that given a desire for land, the wealthier will move to the periphery because they are less affected by the cost of commuting.[4]

Muth's arguments concerning the location of households by income are somewhat similar to Alonso's. Muth assumes the price per unit of housing declines with distance from the CBD. Furthermore the cost of transportation is a positive function of distance from the CBD, the major center of employment. The higher income household, because it consumes more units of housing, will find it advantageous to move farther out from the CBD where the price per unit of housing is cheaper.[5]

A basic assumption in the models of Muth and Alonso is that the CBD is the major focus of activity in the metropolis, especially of employment. Therefore every household locates in such a way that it is in its most advantageous position with reference to the CBD. Of course to make its decision the household must balance conflicting desires: in particular, minimizing transportation cost and hence minimizing distance to the CBD as opposed to maximizing its consumption of housing by moving to the periphery where per unit price of housing is lower. However, the importance given to transportation cost with reference to the CBD in the models of Alonso and Muth directs attention away from the multi-faceted aspects of consumer demand with respect to housing. In fact, as will be argued shortly, we do not need to assume that most households locate themselves with reference to the CBD because their transportation costs to the CBD are important.

The spatial pattern of housing and households at any one period in a city is a complex result of numerous decisions over time. Hence in order to interpret the spatial

---

[1]William Alonso, Location and Land Use (Cambridge: Harvard University Press, 1964), p. 106.

[2]The bid price curve is a function representing the price a household is willing to pay at various distances from the CBD.

[3]Alonso, Location and Land Use, pp. 76-100.

[4]Ibid., pp. 107-9. Alonso is assuming that all workers commute to the CBD.

[5]Richard F. Muth, Cities and Housing (Chicago: University of Chicago Press, 1969), pp. 18-31. The consumer's total expenditure on housing services of his dwelling is the product of the number of units in the dwelling and the price per unit of housing.

pattern at one period we need some generalizations concerning location decisions in previous periods. In the two models to be developed, several simplifying assumptions are made. Assume a small settlement with households congregated around an activity center. This activity center, called the CBD, includes those activities which a household engages in outside the home such as schools, employment, retail stores and entertainment facilities. The settlement is located on a uniform plain which has no inhabitants except those in the settlement. The households are located in a circle surrounding the CBD. However, the settlement is initially so small that there is no differentiation of residential areas by income or housing type. Finally, if a household moves to previously vacant land it always moves to that vacant land which is nearest the activity center.

In the first model I assume that all households prefer to live in new dwellings, partly because the new dwelling will tend to be of better quality than an old dwelling. However, since it is also assumed that cost of dwelling is inversely related to age of dwelling and price paid for housing is positively related to income, then the higher the income of the household the newer the dwelling purchased. With the growth of the settlement's population new housing will be constructed. This construction will take place on the periphery of the settlement because land is cheapest there. However, given my assumptions about age of dwelling and income, the new housing on the periphery will tend to be occupied by the highest income households. Furthermore, since it has been assumed that a household which moves to previously vacant land moves to that vacant land which is nearest the activity center, the peripheral expansion in housing will be uniform in all directions from the CBD. As growth in the settlement proceeds, the highest income households will continue to move to the new housing on the periphery while the lower income households acquire the older housing in the settlement which has depreciated in value. With continued population growth new activity centers will develop to service the population.[1] The relative importance of the CBD as an activity center will decline although in absolute terms it may remain the largest activity center in the city. In such a city household income is positively related to distance from the CBD. To deduce such a spatial pattern no assumptions about marginal costs of transportation have been needed. The only implied assumption employed about transportation was that a household moving to vacant land will move to that vacant land which is nearest an activity center.

In the second model I will retain the assumption that all households prefer to live in new dwellings. However, the assumption that cost of a dwelling is inversely related to

---

[1]For a discussion of the relationship between the spatial pattern of commercial settlements within a city and the spatial distribution of consumers see Brian J. L. Berry, Commercial Structure and Commercial Blight, Department of Geography Research Paper No. 85 (Chicago: Department of Geography, University of Chicago, 1963). In general, the spatial pattern of commercial activities is directly related to the spatial pattern of population.

its age is relaxed. Instead I assume that there is a minimum price for new housing. This price is at a level which excludes the possibility of those households below a certain income purchasing new housing.[1] Thus the new housing on the periphery will be occupied by households whose income is above the level needed to purchase the new housing while the older housing which has depreciated in value to a point which the lowest income households can afford it will be occupied by them. Given growth characteristics described in the first model, household income would be positively related to distance from the CBD, although at a relationship lower than in model one.

The age of dwelling is the only structural characteristic of housing employed in the models. However, other structural characteristics, in particular quality of dwelling, are related to age of dwelling. The newer the dwelling the more likely it will be of sound quality. Furthermore since new housing is constructed for the higher income households and since higher income households consume more housing units per dwelling, the newer housing on the periphery will be larger than the older housing closer to the CBD. Therefore, not only is housing newer with increasing distance from the CBD but it is also better quality and larger housing.

Although black households have been excluded from most housing on the periphery in many cities, housing which they do occupy closer to the CBD may exhibit the same spatial pattern as described in the models except that the new housing would not be present in the black housing market. Thus given the above spatial pattern of housing in a city I hypothesize that

> the median family income (FAMINC) of black households is a positive linear function of distance from the CBD (DISCBD).

This hypothesis is formulated in terms of a simple linear model

$$FAMINC = a + b(DISCBD) \tag{14}$$

The results of the analysis of the model are contained in Table 21.

The regression coefficients are positive and significantly different from zero at the 0.01 level in nine of the sixteen cities.[2] Therefore, the hypothesis that FAMINC of black households is a positive linear function of DISCBD is accepted. However, as an examination of the regression coefficients reveals, all nine significant positive coefficients are for cities which have previously been classified as Non-South. This implies that model 14 only applies to cities outside the South. In fact, the only regression coefficient for a southern city which was significantly different from zero at the 0.01 level was the

---

[1] I believe this assumption is fairly reasonable since the production of housing for low income households by the private sector appears to be nonexistent in the United States.

[2] The probability of observing nine or more significant regression coefficients out of sixteen is $p < 0.0005$.

TABLE 21

RELATION BETWEEN MEDIAN FAMILY INCOME (FAMINC) AND DISTANCE FROM THE CBD (DISCBD)

City	DISCBD[b]	r^2
Atlanta	148.8 (183.9)	.016
Baltimore	1268.0[a] (248.1)	.293
Birmingham	-109.2 (129.3)	.016
Cincinnati	1146.1[a] (352.4)	.325
Columbia	-95.1 (123.3)	.056
Columbus	2377.1[a] (635.9)	.500
Detroit	1416.0[a] (141.0)	.420
Kansas City	1908.1[a] (484.3)	.393
Los Angeles	598.6[a] (197.0)	.094
Memphis	13.0 (142.0)	.000
Milwaukee	4038.7[a] (533.2)	.782
Philadelphia	793.5[a] (132.6)	.251
Richmond	700.2 (561.7)	.066
St. Louis	1081.6[a] (279.5)	.263
Shreveport	-381.2[a] (107.3)	.364
Tampa-St. Petersburg	-16.7 (107.6)	.001

[a]Regression coefficient significant at 0.01 level.

[b]Standard errors of regression coefficients are enclosed in parentheses.

regression coefficient for Shreveport. And the coefficient was negative which means that the spatial pattern is the reverse of the hypothesized pattern. In Shreveport the residential areas with the highest FAMINC are near the CBD and residential areas with the lowest FAMINC are on the periphery of the black settlement. However, as will be seen later, this simple linear model is not the best model for Shreveport.

These results for non-southern cities essentially agree with the findings of Schnore for 1960. He found that income of nonwhites increased with distance from the CBD in a selection of northern and border cities.[1] For southern cities, Schnore reports that his measures of socioeconomic status, income, education, and occupation show an increase with distance from the CBD followed by a decline.[2] The one exception was Atlanta which he claimed fitted the northern and border pattern. However, in my regression analysis for Atlanta no relationship between FAMINC and DISCBD was discovered. The reason for this discrepancy between our results is unclear. One factor may be that Schnore had only four distance zones in Atlanta. This small number may have influenced his results. Another factor may be that Schnore selected tracts with 400 or more nonwhites which were also contiguous to the main areas of nonwhite concentration whereas I selected tracts regardless of their relative location. If the spatial distribution of nonwhite households in southern cities according to socioeconomic status fits the curvilinear pattern suggested by Schnore this might explain the lack of fit of my simple linear model in southern cities. However, Schnore does not offer any explanation for the increase in socioeconomic status with increase in distance from the CBD followed by a decrease in socioeconomic status.

Since the two models postulated earlier do not appear to fit southern cities an alternative model needs to be offered. One avenue of approach would be to assume that southern cities have experienced different growth processes which have led to different spatial patterns of housing than exist in non-southern cities. However, I can think of no reasons why this should be the case. Alternatively, one could suggest that the spatial pattern of white housing in southern cities exhibits the pattern implied by models one or two. However, a peculiar form of white southern constraints on Afro-Americans has led to a

---

[1]Schnore, "Social Class Segregation among Nonwhites in Metropolitan Centers." Schnore combined tracts within radial distance zones of one mile each. He presented only the averages for each distance zone. For an income measure he used per cent with family income of $7000 or more. He found the same spatial pattern for per cent completing high school and per cent employed in white-collar occupations. Schnore did not remove tracts which contained substantial numbers of nonwhites other than Afro-Americans. However, for most cities his results would be relatively unaffected.

[2]The southern cities in Schnore's sample were Atlanta, Birmingham, Memphis, New Orleans, and Richmond.

spatial pattern of black households which is at variance with the pattern implied by the models. To approach the analysis this way would require an assumption that locations in the city are either the property of whites or blacks and neither group affects the demands of the other group for a site. Such an assumption would seem to be unrealistic.

An alternative model which I favor requires only a slight modification of models one and two. This modification takes into account the different histories of black settlement in southern and non-southern cities. The growth of the Afro-American population in non-southern cities originally involved the migration of southern blacks to non-southern cities. The general pattern of black settlement in non-southern cities seems to have involved an initial settlement near the CBD followed by peripheral growth of the black population away from the CBD. Few black households have lived in rural areas outside the South.[1] However, black households do live in rural settlements and on farms surrounding southern cities. In general, a safe assumption is that the black families in these settlements and on the farms are poor. Therefore, assume that the family income of black households increases with distance from the CBD within the continuously built-up area of southern cities. However, low income black households live in settlements on the periphery of this continuously built-up area. Thus I hypothesize a curvilinear model for southern cities in which the median family income (FAMINC) of black households increases with distance from the CBD (DISCBD) and then FAMINC decreases with further distance. Model 15 will be used to test this hypothesis.

$$FAMINC = a + b(DISCBD) + c(DISCBD)^2 \qquad (15)$$

The hypothesis that the FAMINC of black households increases with DISCBD followed by a decrease in FAMINC with increases in DISCBD in southern cities is supported by the data in Table 22. The curvilinear model was significant for six of the seven southern cities, Richmond being the only exception. In all six southern cities for which the model fit, the increase in r^2 with the addition of the $(DISCBD)^2$ term was substantial. However the curvilinear model also was significant in six of the non-southern cities. Los Angeles and Milwaukee were the only non-southern cities for which the $(DISCBD)^2$ term was not significant as expected. In Kansas City the second degree term was significant but the curvature was positive or concave up.

This unexpected discovery that the curvilinear model also fits six non-southern cities may not be very significant. In the first column in Table 23 are recorded the DISCBD at which FAMINC is a maximum for those cities with significant negative curvature. The second column contains the cumulative probability of DISCBD at maximum. The value for each city is the probability of observing a DISCBD less than or equal to the DISCBD at the maximum FAMINC. In other words, the cumulative probability is a rough

---

[1] Frazier, The Negro in the United States, p. 197.

TABLE 22

CURVILINEAR MODEL FOR MEDIAN FAMILY INCOME (FAMINC) AND DISTANCE FROM THE CBD (DISCBD)

City	Independent Variables[d]		r^2	Δr^2[e]	Curvature[f]
	DISCBD	$(DISCBD)^2$			
Atlanta	3071.5[a] (758.4)	-904.5[a] (229.6)	.296	.280	–
Baltimore	6122.6[a] (661.4)	-1452.5[a] (190.5)	.635	.342	–
Birmingham	1622.3[a] (513.8)	-544.5[a] (157.4)	.226	.210	–
Cincinnati	4649.8[a] (1358.1)	-1276.6[b] (481.6)	.494	.169	–
Columbia	1595.8[b] (536.2)	-458.1[b] (143.2)	.558	.502	–
Columbus	8053.0[a] (2595.2)	-4400.9[b] (1964.7)	.639	.139	–
Detroit	6115.0[a] (519.1)	-1270.8[a] (137.1)	.643	.223	–
Kansas City	-5245.2[c] (3046.4)	3351.5[b] (1412.1)	.512	.119	+
Los Angeles	2987.2[b] (1492.6)	-577.3 (357.7)	.120	.026	
Memphis	2946.3[a] (405.9)	-900.4[a] (121.2)	.574	.574	–
Milwaukee	10050.0[c] (5362.3)	-3154.4 (2800.2)	.799	.017	
Philadelphia	3741.7[a] (468.2)	-903.2[a] (139.2)	.464	.213	–
Richmond	3376.6 (2776.2)	-1465.7 (1488.8)	.107	.041	
St. Louis	4820.8[a] (1092.7)	-1134.7[a] (322.9)	.433	.170	–
Shreveport	1174.2[b] (421.3)	-424.0[a] (112.5)	.621	.257	–
Tampa-St. Petersburg	1199.4[b] (546.7)	-336.5[b] (148.8)	.222	.221	–

[a]Regression coefficient significant at 0.01 level.

[b]Regression coefficient significant at 0.05 level.

[c]Regression coefficient significant at 0.10 level.

[d]Standard error of regression coefficients are enclosed in parentheses.

[e]Increase in r^2 with addition of $(DISCBD)^2$ term.

[f]Curvature of function with respect to DISCBD axis. + is concave up and – is concave down.

TABLE 23

ANALYSIS OF DISTANCE FROM THE CBD (DISCBD) AT MAXIMUM MEDIAN FAMILY INCOME (FAMINC) FOR CITIES WITH SIGNIFICANT NEGATIVE CURVATURE

City	DISCBD at Maximum	Cumulative Probability of DISCBD at Maximum
Atlanta	1.698	.72
Baltimore	2.108	.97
Birmingham	1.490	.45
Cincinnati	1.821	.89
Columbia	1.742	.64
Columbus	.915	.92
Detroit	2.406	.94
Memphis	1.636	.63
Philadelphia	2.071	.88
St. Louis	2.124	.90
Shreveport	1.385	.36
Tampa-St. Petersburg	1.782	.77

measure of the proportion of black residential areas in the city lying between the CBD and the DISCBD at the maximum FAMINC. The cumulative probability for all southern cities is lower than the cumulative probability for all non-southern. This means that the DISCBD at which FAMINC is a maximum is relatively closer to the CBD in southern cities than in non-southern cities. In fact the lowest cumulative probability for non-southern cities is Philadelphia with 0.88. Thus the maximum on the curves for non-southern cities occurs at a DISCBD beyond which few black residential areas are located. Hence the curvilinear model for non-southern cities is not meaningful. The curvature which does exist probably identifies the lower FAMINC in the few black residential areas located in satellite cities of the main central city.

In the two models I have postulated that the spatial distribution of black households by income in a city is related to the spatial distribution of housing with reference to the CBD. In particular, it has been suggested that quality of housing (PCSOND) and size of dwelling (MROOMS)[1] should increase with DISCBD, age of dwelling (PCPR39) should decrease with DISCBD, and because of the relationship of the above with median value of owner occupied units (VALOWN) and median rent of renter occupied units (MDRENT), both VALOWN and MDRENT will increase with DISCBD. Table 24 contains the correlation coefficients of the above housing variables with DISCBD. In general, the correlation coefficients are similar to what were postulated. The one exception is VALOWN. It was

---

[1]MROOMS stands for median number of rooms in dwelling units in a residential area.

TABLE 24

CORRELATION OF DISTANCE FROM THE CBD (DISCBD) WITH PER CENT SOUND UNITS (PCSOND), MEDIAN NUMBER OF ROOMS (MROOMS), PER CENT OCCUPIED UNITS BUILT 1939 OR EARLIER (PCPR39), MEDIAN VALUE OF OWNER OCCUPIED UNITS (VALOWN), AND MEDIAN RENT OF RENTER OCCUPIED UNITS (MDRENT)

City	PCSOND	MROOMS	PCPR39	VALOWN	MDRENT
Atlanta	.018	.395[a]	-.511[a]	-.469[a]	-.166
Baltimore	.481[a]	.248[b]	-.295[a]	.576[a]	.443[a]
Birmingham	-.222	.347[a]	-.384[a]	-.740[a]	-.663[a]
Cincinnati	.656[a]	.855[a]	-.453[b]	.273	.684[a]
Columbia	-.315	.693[a]	-.215	-.742[a]	-.725[a]
Columbus	.684[a]	.602[a]	-.664[a]	.322	.214
Detroit	.492[a]	.230[a]	-.500[a]	.287[a]	.480[a]
Kansas City	.702[a]	.620[a]	-.178	.817[a]	.729[a]
Los Angeles	.250[a]	.394[a]	-.755[a]	-.140	.578[a]
Memphis	-.218	.586[a]	-.651[a]	-.610[a]	-.241
Milwaukee	.659[a]	.861[a]	.395	.632[a]	.841[a]
Philadelphia	.291[a]	.500[a]	-.344[a]	.470[a]	.497[a]
Richmond	.302	.628[a]	-.026	-.037	.298
St. Louis	.331[b]	.560[a]	-.023	.191	.355[b]
Shreveport	-.636[a]	.559[a]	-.386[b]	-.672[a]	-.872[a]
Tampa-St. Petersburg	.040	.165	-.333	-.513[a]	-.293

[a]Correlation coefficient significant at 0.01 level.

[b]Correlation coefficient significant at 0.05 level.

anticipated that the significant coefficients would be positive. However, only five were positive while six were negative. Since I have argued that the spatial distribution of black households with respect to the CBD is a function of the spatial distribution of housing, then I hypothesize that there is no relationship between median family income (FAMINC) and DISCBD when the housing variables are held constant. The following model will be used to examine this hypothesis.

$$FAMINC = a + b(PCSOND) + c(MROOMS) + d(PCPR39) + e(VALOWN) + f(MDRENT) + g(DISCBD) \tag{16}$$

Since the interest is in the partial correlation between FAMINC and DISCBD, this and the simple correlation are the only correlations contained in Table 25.

Clearly, the hypothesis stated above applies chiefly to non-southern cities since these cities were the only cities which contained a significant positive linear relationship between FAMINC and DISCBD. As is evident from Table 25, only two of the partial correlations between FAMINC and DISCBD in non-southern cities are significant and positive at the 0.05 level. Hence there is some support for the contention that the spatial pattern of

TABLE 25

SIMPLE CORRELATION BETWEEN MEDIAN FAMILY INCOME (FAMINC) AND DISTANCE FROM THE CBD (DISCBD) AND PARTIAL CORRELATION BETWEEN FAMINC AND DISCBD HOLDING PER CENT SOUND UNITS (PCSOND), MEDIAN NUMBER OF ROOMS (MROOMS), PER CENT OCCUPIED UNITS BUILT 1939 OR EARLIER (PCPR39), MEDIAN VALUE OF OWNER OCCUPIED UNITS (VALOWN), AND MEDIAN RENT OF RENTER OCCUPIED UNITS (MDRENT) CONSTANT

City	DISCBD[c]	r^2
Atlanta	.127 -.043	.016 .807
Baltimore	.541[a] .070	.293 .869
Birmingham	-.125 .179	.016 .644
Cincinnati	.570[a] -.097	.325 .952
Columbia	-.237 -.331	.056 .662
Columbus	.707[a] .820[a]	.500 .952
Detroit	.648[a] .428[a]	.420 .821
Kansas City	.627[a] -.459[b]	.393 .919
Los Angeles	.307[a] -.159	.094 .685
Memphis	.014 -.270	.000 .710
Milwaukee	.884[a] .528	.782 .924
Philadelphia	.501[a] .038	.251 .835
Richmond	.257 -.052	.066 .729
St. Louis	.513[a] .278	.263 .822
Shreveport	-.604[a] -.304	.364 .862
Tampa-St. Petersburg	-.036 -.055	.001 .815

[a]Significant at 0.01 level.

[b]Significant at 0.05 level.

[c]Simple correlation on first line and partial correlation on second line for each city.

black households according to FAMINC with respect to the CBD is related to the spatial distribution of housing in the city. When the effects of housing are removed, little or no significant relationship between median family income (FAMINC) and distance from the CBD (DISCBD) remains. Of course this conclusion applies chiefly to non-southern cities. In southern cities the spatial distribution of households by FAMINC was essentially a curvilinear function of DISCBD. As expected, the partial correlations between FAMINC and DISCBD were non-significant in southern cities.

CHAPTER V

RELATIONS BETWEEN FAMILY CHARACTERISTICS AND HOUSING

Are there also relationships between the spatial distribution of family characteristics and the spatial distribution of housing characteristics, assuming a fixed spatial pattern of housing? We now turn to this second facet of the manner in which black households are distributed among black residential areas.

Life Cycle and Housing

The previous review of literature on residential choice suggests that the type of housing preferred by a family varies with changes in the life cycle of the family. Single people and young childless couples with smaller demands for space prefer apartments. Couples with children, however, prefer single family dwellings which provide extra interior space as well as yards for children to play in. Specific evidence concerning the relationship between life cycle and housing among black households is meager. Frazier's study of Chicago is one of the few such studies. He found a positive relationship between proportion of children in the population and the stabilization of family life. He implies that the most stable forms of family life existed in the area of single family dwellings.[1] In spite of the meager evidence on individual black household behavior the general studies of residential choice strongly suggest that the type of housing a black household occupies should be related to the life cycle of the household. Of course an important provision is that the type of housing demanded by the household must be available. Also, the decision to live in a single family dwelling is partly influenced by household income. The single family dwelling is frequently larger and costs more to maintain than an apartment.

Therefore, assuming that the preference for living in a single family dwelling increases with the number of children in the family, that similar types of housing are constructed in relatively close proximity, and that all types of housing are available to black households, I hypothesize that the

---

[1] Frazier, The Negro Family in Chicago, pp. 136-46.

per cent of the population under 18 years (PCPP18) in a black residential area is positively related to the per cent single family dwellings (PCSFDW) when median family income (FAMINC) is held constant.

The model which will be examined is

$$PCPP18 = a + b(PCSFDW) + c(FAMINC) \quad (17)$$

The results of the analysis of model 17 are contained in Table 26.

Looking first at the simple correlation between PCPP18 and PCSFDW we can observe that the correlation is positive and significant at the 0.10 level in eight cities.[1] When FAMINC is held constant, the partial correlation between PCPP18 and PCSFDW is positive and significant at the 0.10 level in nine cities. In thirteen of the sixteen cities the correlation between PCPP18 and PCSFDW increased in the direction hypothesized when FAMINC was held constant. Thus there is some evidence for tentatively accepting the hypothesis which states, in effect, that when the factor of income is removed, large (small) proportions of young children are found in residential areas with large (small) proportions of single family dwellings. However, the relationship is not so strong as to imply that this is a dominant characteristic of black residential areas. The r^2 values for model 17 are not very high in most of the cities. Judging from the distribution of significant partial correlations between PCPP18 and PCSFDW among southern and non-southern cities, it appears that the hypothesis holds equally well for both groups of cities. The negative partial correlation between PCPP18 and FAMINC in fourteen of the cities when PCSFDW is held constant might be explained in at least two ways. First, children come at an early stage in the life cycle of a family when the father's income is at the lowest level in his career. As the number of children under 18 years declines the father's income is usually rising. Therefore given a spatial variation in households by income and holding dwelling type constant, higher PCPP18 are found in those residential areas with lower FAMINC. Alternatively, the same conclusion could follow if higher income families have fewer children than lower income families.

Another related way of viewing the relationship between life cycle and housing is to examine owner occupancy. Several authors have suggested that there is an increase in rates of home ownership with increases in age and size of family.[2] However, it was reported in the last chapter that per cent owner occupancy (PCONOC) was positively related to FAMINC among black residential areas. Therefore, the relationship between FAMINC and PCONOC will be controlled. Assuming that black residential areas vary by proportion owner occupancy and that the larger the number of young children in the family

---

[1]The probability of obtaining eight or more significant correlations out of sixteen at the 0.10 level is $p < 0.0005$.

[2]Maisel and Winnick, "Family Housing Expenditures: Elusive Laws and Intrusive Variances," p. 395; and Duncan and Hauser, Housing a Metropolis--Chicago, p. 236.

TABLE 26

SIMPLE CORRELATION BETWEEN PER CENT POPULATION UNDER 18 YEARS (PCPP18) AND PER CENT SINGLE FAMILY DWELLINGS (PCSFDW) AND PARTIAL CORRELATION OF PCPP18 WITH PCSFDW AND MEDIAN FAMILY INCOME (FAMINC)

City	Independent Variables[d]		r^2
	PCSFDW	FAMINC	
Atlanta	.049		.002
	.272[c]	-.381[b]	.147
Baltimore	.305[b]		.093
	.440[a]	-.473[a]	.296
Birmingham	.584[a]		.341
	.601[a]	-.196	.366
Cincinnati	.296		.088
	.685[a]	-.747[a]	.597
Columbia	.535[c]		.286
	.563[c]	-.214	.319
Columbus	.350		.122
	.330	.051	.125
Detroit	.307[a]		.094
	.417[a]	-.327[a]	.191
Kansas City	.434[b]		.188
	.087	.297	.260
Los Angeles	.263[b]		.069
	.283[a]	-.110	.080
Memphis	.343[b]		.117
	.387[b]	-.244	.170
Milwaukee	-.098		.010
	.137	-.584[b]	.347
Philadelphia	.115		.013
	.271[a]	-.315[a]	.111
Richmond	-.115		.013
	.040	-.472[b]	.233
St. Louis	.167		.028
	.219	-.476[a]	.248
Shreveport	.368[c]		.135
	.314	-.315	.221
Tampa-St. Petersburg	-.297		.088
	-.050	-.348	.199

[a]Significant at 0.01 level. [b]Significant at 0.05 level.

[c]Significant at 0.10 level.

[d]Partial correlations on second line for each city.

the more likely the household will purchase its dwelling, I hypothesize that PCPP18 is positively related to PCONOC holding FAMINC constant. The model which will be used is

$$PCPP18 = a + b(PCONOC) + c(FAMINC) \quad (18)$$

The results of the analysis of model 18 are contained in Table 27.

When FAMINC is held constant, the partial correlation between PCPP18 and PCONOC is positive and significant at the 0.10 level in nine cities. Hence the hypothesis is partially supported. In fifteen of the cities the correlation between PCPP18 and PCONOC increased when FAMINC was held constant, which seems to indicate that the correlation between PCPP18 and PCONOC is partly obscured by the close tie between FAMINC and PCONOC among black residential areas. For example, residential areas which contain young families who have low incomes are also likely to have low proportions of owner occupancy. An interesting result for which I have no explanation is that the hypothesis is supported in six of the seven cities in the southern category and in only three of the nine cities in the non-southern category. The negative partial correlation between PCPP18 and FAMINC for fifteen cities could be interpreted in the same manner as the negative partial correlation between PCPP18 and FAMINC in model 17.

It has been suggested that families with children prefer to live in single family dwellings. Furthermore, some evidence has been presented which suggests that larger proportions of children are found in black residential areas with larger proportions of single family dwellings. Therefore, since density of population has been shown to decline negative exponentially with distance from the CBD[1] and by implication higher proportions of single family dwellings will be found with increasing distance from the CBD, I hypothesize that

> the per cent population under 18 (PCPP18) of a black residential area is a positive linear function of distance from the CBD (DISCBD).

Expressed in functional notation

$$PCPP18 = a + b(DISCBD) \quad (19)$$

Model 19 is significant at least at the 0.10 level for ten of the cities listed in Table 28. Therefore there is some tendency for PCPP18 of a black residential area to increase with DISCBD. All seven cities in the southern category and only three of the nine cities in the non-southern category had significant regression coefficients. Thus the simple linear model 19 definitely seems to apply to southern cities but it is doubtful if model 19 is generally applicable to non-southern cities.

The temptation may be to argue that residential segregation of Afro-Americans is lower in southern cities than in non-southern cities and therefore black households have access to all types of housing, especially on the periphery. However, segregation indexes

---

[1]Muth, Cities and Housing, pp. 141-44.

TABLE 27

SIMPLE CORRELATION BETWEEN PER CENT POPULATION UNDER 18 YEARS (PCPP18) AND PER CENT OWNER OCCUPIED UNITS (PCONOC) AND PARTIAL CORRELATION OF PCPP18 WITH PCONOC AND MEDIAN FAMILY INCOME (FAMINC)

City	Independent Variables[d]		r^2
	PCONOC	FAMINC	
Atlanta	-.004		.000
	.367[b]	-.451[a]	.204
Baltimore	-.234[c]		.055
	.201	-.338[a]	.163
Birmingham	.485[a]		.235
	.518[a]	-.222	.273
Cincinnati	.014		.000
	.601[a]	-.717[a]	.515
Columbia	.821[a]		.674
	.915[a]	-.708[b]	.837
Columbus	.406		.165
	.411	-.149	.184
Detroit	.200[b]		.040
	.458[a]	-.441[a]	.227
Kansas City	.542[a]		.294
	.236	.044	.296
Los Angeles	.406[a]		.165
	.588[a]	-.466[a]	.346
Memphis	.224		.050
	.395[a]	-.363[b]	.176
Milwaukee	-.407[c]		.166
	.248	-.501[b]	.376
Philadelphia	-.132		.017
	.091	-.179[c]	.049
Richmond	-.083		.007
	.384[c]	-.584[a]	.346
St. Louis	-.078		.006
	.253	-.506[a]	.260
Shreveport	.174		.030
	.380[c]	-.488[b]	.261
Tampa-St. Petersburg	-.053		.003
	.378	-.556[b]	.311

[a]Significant at 0.01 level. [b]Significant at 0.05 level.

[c]Significant at 0.10 level.

[d]Partial correlations on second line for each city.

TABLE 28

RELATION BETWEEN PER CENT POPULATION UNDER 18 (PCPP18) AND DISTANCE FROM THE CBD (DISCBD)

City	Independent Variable[c] DISCBD	r^2
Atlanta	.0637[a] (.0138)	.348
Baltimore	-.0119 (.0162)	.009
Birmingham	.0463[a] (.0070)	.495
Cincinnati	.0250 (.0309)	.029
Columbia	.0410[a] (.0127)	.512
Columbus	.1051 (.0671)	.149
Detroit	.0221[b] (.0133)	.019
Kansas City	.0625[b] (.0333)	.128
Los Angeles	.1347[a] (.0146)	.490
Memphis	.0501[a] (.0115)	.311
Milwaukee	-.0597 (.0577)	.063
Philadelphia	.0001 (.0086)	.000
Richmond	.0859[b] (.0443)	.146
St. Louis	-.0146 (.0189)	.014
Shreveport	.0347[a] (.0087)	.418
Tampa-St. Petersburg	.0312[b] (.0152)	.182

[a]Regression coefficient significant at 0.01 level.

[b]Regression coefficient significant at 0.10 level.

[c]Standard errors of regression coefficients are enclosed in parentheses.

which the Taeubers computed for central cities indicate that Afro-Americans are highly segregated in all cities of the United States.[1] The Taeubers' segregation indexes for the central cities of the SMSA's included in this study are reproduced in Table 29. The indexes clearly indicate that Afro-Americans and whites are highly segregated in all sixteen cities.[2] Thus residential segregation per se does not seem to explain the findings in Table 28. In fact the mean segregation index for the southern cities in Table 29 is 95.6 which is higher than the mean for non-southern cities which was 87.5.

TABLE 29

SEGREGATION INDEXES

Central City	Index[a]
Atlanta	93.6
Baltimore	89.6
Birmingham	92.8
Cincinnati	89.0
Columbia	94.1
Columbus	85.3
Detroit	84.5
Kansas City	91.2[b]
Los Angeles	81.8
Memphis	92.0
Milwaukee	88.1
Philadelphia	87.1
Richmond	94.8
St. Louis	90.5
Shreveport	95.9
Tampa-St. Petersburg	95.8[c]

Source: Karl E. Taueber and Alma F. Taueber, Negroes in Cities (Chicago: Aldine Publishing Company, 1965), Table 1, pp. 32-34.

[a]Index is for central cities and hence is not directly comparable to my cities.

[b]The value is an average of separate indexes the Taeubers gave for Kansas City, Kansas (91.5) and Kansas City, Missouri (90.8).

[c]An average for Tampa (94.5) and St. Petersburg (97.1).

---

[1]Taeuber and Taeuber, Negroes in Cities, p. 35.

[2]The index of residential segregation ranges from 0 to 100. The higher the index the higher the degree of segregation. See Taeuber and Taeuber, Negroes in Cities, p. 30.

Although Afro-Americans are highly segregated from whites in southern cities, Afro-Americans in these cities may have access to a wider range of housing farther from the CBD than do Afro-Americans in non-southern cities. In fact, this seems to be the case. In the previous chapter it was shown that distance indexes for southern cities were greater than distance indexes for non-southern cities.[1] This means that controlling for SMSA population size, Afro-American residential areas tend to be found at greater distances from the CBD in southern cities than in non-southern cities. By implication, the black housing market in southern cities includes a larger proportion of housing in low density areas towards the periphery of the SMSA's than does the black housing market in non-southern cities. Since most black households obtain housing within the black housing market, the greater the spatial spread of black residential areas from the CBD the greater the possibility of families with children finding suitable housing in low density areas. Although the above distance index is admittedly crude I hypothesize that the higher the distance index of a city in Table 18, the stronger the relationship between PCPP18 and DISCBD measured by the r^2 in Table 28.

To test this hypothesis the gamma statistic, suggested by Goodman and Kruskal, was computed.[2] The distance indexes were ranked from one (lowest) to sixteen (highest). The same operation was carried out for the r^2 values relating PCPP18 and DISCBD. The gamma statistic is a measure of how much more probable it is to get the same ordering of both variables versus a different ordering of both variables for a randomly selected pair. For the sample of cities the gamma measuring the ordering of the distance index and r^2 was .53. Thus the probability is .53 that the ordering of a pair (distance index and r^2 for a city) is the same. This probability is a measure of the monotone relationship between the distance index and r^2. From the computation of the gamma statistic it was observed that the variables for Los Angeles were extremely divergent. Los Angeles was ranked 14 on r^2 and only 2 on the distance index. No other city diverged this much. Los Angeles was dropped from the analysis and the gamma statistic was re-computed. This time gamma was .72. Thus, with the exception of Los Angeles, there seems to be evidence that the r^2 relating per cent population under 18 (PCPP18) and distance from the CBD (DISCBD) _and_ the distance index are monotone increasing. The probability is .72 that a randomly selected city has the same rank on both the r^2 and the distance index.

This result can be interpreted to mean that the spatial variation of the black housing market is a factor in setting up the possibility of black households finding housing in a

---

[1]Table 18 in the previous chapter contains the distance indexes.

[2]Leo A. Goodman and William H. Kruskal, "Measures of Association for Cross-Classifications," _Journal of the American Statistical Association_, XLIX (December, 1954), 747-54.

residential area which meets the needs appropriate to their particular stage in life cycle. If the assumption is correct that the greater the number of children in a black family the farther from the CBD the family wishes to live, then the success of a black household in expressing this desire is dependent upon existing spatial spread of the black residential areas. In southern cities black residential areas are relatively scattered about the cities and located in the low density areas on the peripheries. Hence black households with children can find housing appropriate to their needs while households without children can of course live near the CBD. However, in most non-southern cities black residential areas are only found close to the CBD. Therefore, black households with children cannot find housing appropriate to their needs.

Although the simple linear model 19 did not give significant results for six of the cities in the non-southern category, this does not necessarily imply that there are no regularities in the spatial distribution of PCPP18 with respect to the CBD. An alternative model for non-southern cities can be specified. The assumption that the larger the number of young children in a black family the farther the household wants to live from the CBD will be retained, with the added qualification that the poorest families have large numbers of children. Furthermore, because of their low income these families can only purchase housing close to the CBD where dwelling units are small, old, and deteriorated and hence low cost. Low cost public housing is also located near the CBD and the poor families may live in them. Therefore the spatial pattern implied by this model means that per cent population under 18 (PCPP18) would be high near the CBD followed by a decline away from the CBD which in turn is followed by an increase in PCPP18 towards the periphery of the city.[1] A graphic portrayal of this model is contained in Figure 7. This model can also be expressed in the following manner

$$PCPP18 = a + b(DISCBD) + c(DISCBD)^2 \qquad (20)$$

The results of the analysis of the hypothesized curvilinear model for non-southern cities are contained in Table 30.

The hypothesized curvature is significant in only three of the nine cities in the non-southern category: Baltimore, Kansas City, and St. Louis. For these three cities the curvature is positive or concave up as diagramed in Figure 7. The DISCBD for which PCPP18 is a minimum is presented in Table 31. For Baltimore and St. Louis the minimum point is farther from the CBD than the mean DISCBD and the reverse is true for Kansas City. If the rationale for the simple linear model is reasonable then it could be inferred that black households located between the CBD and the DISCBD at the minimum PCPP18 in the curvilinear model are not in the location which they prefer, given the presence of young children in the household.

---

[1]This model is also partially implied in Frazier's study of black families in Chicago. See Frazier, The Negro Family in Chicago, pp. 136-46.

TABLE 30

CURVILINEAR MODEL FOR PER CENT POPULATION UNDER 18 (PCPP18)

City	Independent Variables[d]		r^2	Increase[e] in r^2	Curvature[f]
	DISCBD	$(DISCBD)^2$			
Atlanta	.1039 (.0668)	-.0124 (.0202)	.355	.007	
Baltimore	-.1212[b] (.0584)	.0327[c] (.0168)	.065	.056	+
Birmingham	.1107[a] (.0296)	-.0203[b] (.0091)	.546	.051	-
Cincinnati	-.0829 (.1356)	.0393 (.0481)	.059	.030	
Columbia	.2164[a] (.0545)	-.0475[a] (.0146)	.776	.264	-
Columbus	-.0291 (.3202)	.1040 (.2424)	.161	.012	
Detroit	-.0723 (.0618)	.0255 (.0163)	.037	.018	
Kansas City	-.3257 (.2187)	.1819[c] (.1014)	.235	.107	+
Los Angeles	.4134[a] (.1080)	-.0674[b] (.0259)	.526	.036	-
Memphis	.0531 (.0504)	-.0009 (.0150)	.311	.000	
Milwaukee	.0996 (.6029)	-.0836 (.3148)	.067	.004	
Philadelphia	-.0236 (.0359)	.0073 (.0107)	.004	.004	
Richmond	.1312 (.2239)	-.0248 (.1201)	.148	.002	
St. Louis	-.2009[b] (.0790)	.0565[b] (.0234)	.137	.123	+
Shreveport	.0732 (.0436)	-.0105 (.0116)	.439	.021	
Tampa-St. Petersburg	.1281 (.0842)	-.0268 (.0229)	.239	.057	

[a]Regression coefficient significant at 0.01 level.

[b]Regression coefficient significant at 0.05 level.

[c]Regression coefficient significant at 0.10 level.

[d]Standard errors of regression coefficients are enclosed in parentheses.

[e]Increase in r^2 with addition of $(DISCBD)^2$ term.

[f]Curvature of function with respect to DISCBD axis: + is concave up and - is concave down.

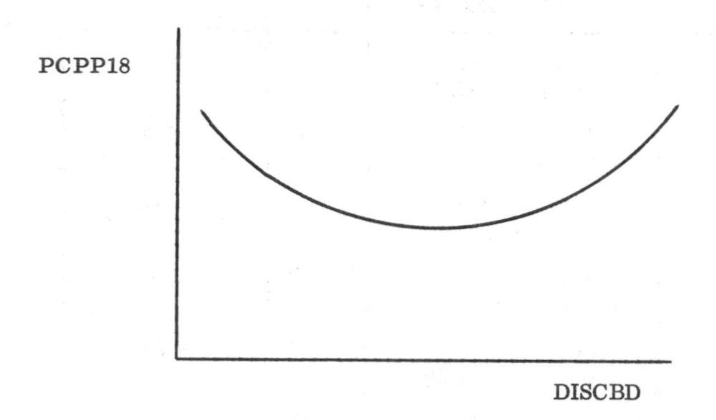

Fig. 7.--Curvilinear Model for Non-Southern Cities

TABLE 31

ANALYSIS OF CURVATURE IN MODEL 20

Curvature: Concave Up (+)	DISCBD at Minimum[a]	Mean DISCBD
Baltimore	1.854	1.216
Kansas City	.895	1.071
St. Louis	1.777	1.496

Curvature: Concave Down (-)	DISCBD at Maximum[a]	Mean DISCBD
Birmingham	2.731	1.591
Columbia	2.277	1.367
Los Angeles	3.068	2.002

[a]Solved by setting first derivative of regression equation $PCPP18 = a + b(DISCBD) + c(DISCBD)^2$ equal to zero.

The second degree term is also significant but negative or concave down in Birmingham, Columbia, and Los Angeles. For Los Angeles the curvature is the opposite of the hypothesized curvature. The spatial pattern of PCPP18 in Los Angeles is close to the pattern in southern cities. In fact the simple linear model was also significant for Los Angeles. A comparison of the DISCBD at the maximum PCPP18 with the mean DISCBD (Table 31) indicates that the maximum is located substantially farther from the CBD than the mean DISCBD for Birmingham, Columbia, and Los Angeles. Hence the decline in PCPP18 probably does not occur until the periphery of the city is reached and is therefore not especially meaningful.

Husband-Wife Family Units and Housing

The presence or absence of husband or wife, although not developed in the literature on residential choice, would seem to be an important factor in residential decisions. The needs and resources of the household vary depending upon whether or not the husband and/or wife are present. For example, if a husband is not in the household the earnings of a family will, in all likelihood, be low. These earnings influence the amount and type of housing the household is capable of purchasing. Therefore, given spatial variation in housing, we might expect that indicators of family structure such as husband-wife combinations would also vary systematically among residential areas.

Frazier, in his study of black families in Chicago in 1920, seemed to imply that rates of female heads of families were inversely related to home ownership among residential areas.[1] Such a pattern would seem to be logically consistent with ideas in the residential choice literature. Where males are heads of households family income is probably higher and hence capability of owning a home is greater than in households where females are the heads. If there is spatial variation in owner occupancy a pattern such as Frazier observed could exist. Per cent households which are husband-wife households (WIV/HD) will be used as a measure of marital status. Therefore I hypothesize that

> the per cent households which are husband wife households (WIV/HD) in a black residential area is positively related to the per cent owner occupied dwellings (PCONOC).

WIV/HD and PCONOC are positively and significantly correlated at the 0.01 level in all sixteen cities. See Table 32. Since most of the correlations in Table 32 appear similar I hypothesize that all of them are estimates of the same population value. To test this hypothesis the test of homogeneity of k values of r described in Edwards will be employed.[2] The null hypothesis is that all sixteen correlations in Table 32 are homo-

---

[1]Frazier, The Negro Family in Chicago, pp. 136-46.

[2]Edwards, Experimental Design in Psychological Research, pp. 83-85.

TABLE 32

CORRELATION BETWEEN PER CENT HOUSEHOLDS WHICH ARE HUSBAND-WIFE HOUSEHOLDS (WIV/HD) AND PER CENT OWNER OCCUPIED UNITS (PCONOC)

City	r[a]
Atlanta	.839
Baltimore	.883
Birmingham	.586
Cincinnati	.905
Columbia	.891
Columbus	.814
Detroit	.889
Kansas City	.948
Los Angeles	.900
Memphis	.771
Milwaukee	.846
Philadelphia	.875
Richmond	.835
St. Louis	.775
Shreveport	.658
Tampa-St. Petersburg	.838

[a]All correlation coefficients significant at 0.01 level.

geneous. A chi square of 42.6 with 15 degrees of freedom was obtained. Using a 0.01 level of significance this means that the probability is less than 0.01 that the sixteen correlations are estimates of the same population correlation. However, an examination of Table 32 reveals that the correlation between WIV/HD and PCONOC for Birmingham is substantially less than the correlations for the other cities and hence Birmingham may represent an extreme case. Therefore the same test as above was computed with the exclusion of Birmingham. This time the chi square is 25.0 with 14 degrees of freedom. Using a 0.01 level of significance the null hypothesis that the fifteen correlations are estimates of the same population correlation cannot be rejected. Therefore the degree of correlation between WIV/HD and PCONOC among black residential areas is relatively the same among fifteen cities in the sample. Thus the spatial pattern which Frazier described in Chicago in 1920 appears to hold for black residential areas in my sample of cities in 1960.

However, as indicated above, the presence of a husband in the household is likely to affect family income which in turn influences decisions about owning a home. Alternatively one might suggest that higher income families tend to own their homes and at the same time in higher income families both husband and wife are present. In any case the tie between WIV/HD and PCONOC may only occur because median family income (FAMINC) is an intermediate factor. Therefore to test whether or not there is any tie between per cent households with both husband and wife present (WIV/HD) and per cent owner occupied dwellings (PCONOC) when FAMINC is held constant, the following model is employed:

$$WIV/HD = a + b(PCONOC) + c(FAMINC) \quad (21)$$

The results of the analysis of model 21 are contained in Table 33.

With the exception of Milwaukee, all of the partial correlations between WIV/HD and PCONOC holding FAMINC constant are positive and significant at the 0.01 level. This finding means that black residential areas vary systematically according to WIV/HD and PCONOC regardless of the variation in FAMINC.

In his discussion of black families in Chicago Frazier also implies that rates of husband-wife pairs increases with increases in the distance of zones from the CBD. Frazier associated increases in the proportion of men married in successive zones with increasing stabilization of family life.[1] This variation in family life seemed to correspond to variation in housing quality and economic status of the residents.[2] Frazier's findings can be interpreted in terms of residential choice. Assume that higher income families tend to have both husband and wife present. Therefore, higher income families tend to move farther from the CBD than lower income families because the housing demanded by the higher income family is located farther from the CBD (for reasons discussed in the previous chapter).

Given spatial variation in housing I hypothesize that the proportion of households which are husband-wife households (WIV/HD) of a black residential area is a positive function of distance from the CBD (DISCBD). Since median family income (FAMINC) of a residential area is positively associated with both WIV/HD and DISCBD, FAMINC will be held constant to see if variation in WIV/HD with respect to the CBD is inseparable from the variation in FAMINC. The model employed is

$$WIV/HD = a + b(DISCBD) + c(FAMINC) \quad (22)$$

The results of the analysis of model 22 are contained in Table 34.

As is evident, the simple correlation between WIV/HD and DISCBD is significant at least at the 0.05 level in fifteen of the sixteen cities. When FAMINC is included in the analysis (Model 22) the partial correlation between WIV/HD and DISCBD is significant at the 0.01 level in thirteen cities. Thus, even when median family income (FAMINC) is held constant, black residential areas with higher per cent households with both husband and wife present (WIV/HD) tend to be found farther from the CBD than black residential areas with lower WIV/HD. This finding may occur because the spatial variation of WIV/HD with respect to the CBD is related to housing variables which are not completely

---

[1]Frazier, The Negro Family in Chicago, pp. 120-21.

[2]*Ibid.*, p. 101.

TABLE 33

SIMPLE CORRELATION BETWEEN PER CENT HOUSEHOLDS WHICH ARE HUSBAND-WIFE HOUSEHOLDS (WIV/HD) AND PER CENT OWNER OCCUPIED UNITS (PCONOC) AND PARTIAL CORRELATION OF WIV/HD WITH PCONOC AND MEDIAN FAMILY INCOME (FAMINC)

City	Independent Variables[c]		r^2
	PCONOC	FAMINC	
Atlanta	.839[a]		.704
	.588[a]	.339[b]	.738
Baltimore	.883[a]		.780
	.461[a]	.426[a]	.820
Birmingham	.586[a]		.343
	.569[a]	.527[a]	.525
Cincinnati	.905[a]		.820
	.795[a]	.579[a]	.880
Columbia	.891[a]		.794
	.877[a]	.424	.831
Columbus	.814[a]		.663
	.693[a]	.446	.730
Detroit	.889[a]		.791
	.764[a]	.212[b]	.800
Kansas City	.948[a]		.898
	.702[a]	.493[b]	.923
Los Angeles	.900[a]		.810
	.787[a]	.310[a]	.828
Memphis	.771[a]		.595
	.685[a]	.065	.596
Milwaukee	.846[a]		.716
	.352	.514[b]	.791
Philadelphia	.875[a]		.765
	.526[a]	.355[a]	.795
Richmond	.835[a]		.697
	.691[a]	.277	.720
St. Louis	.775[a]		.601
	.650[a]	.718[a]	.807
Shreveport	.658[a]		.433
	.791[a]	-.594[a]	.633
Tampa-St. Petersburg	.838[a]		.702
	.672[a]	.497[b]	.776

[a]Significant at 0.01 level. [b]Significant at 0.05 level.

[c]Simple correlation is on first line for each city and partial correlation on second line.

TABLE 34

SIMPLE CORRELATION BETWEEN PER CENT HOUSEHOLDS WHICH ARE HUSBAND-WIFE HOUSEHOLDS (WIV/HD) AND DISTANCE FROM THE CBD (DISCBD) AND PARTIAL CORRELATION OF WIV/HD WITH DISCBD AND MEDIAN FAMILY INCOME (FAMINC)

City	Independent Variables[c]		r^2
	DISCBD	FAMINC	
Atlanta	.542[a]		.294
	.706[a]	.846[a]	.799
Baltimore	.508[a]		.258
	.082	.833[a]	.773
Birmingham	.485[a]		.235
	.666[a]	.699[a]	.609
Cincinnati	.845[a]		.714
	.804[a]	.773[a]	.885
Columbia	.525[b]		.276
	.780[a]	.778[a]	.713
Columbus	.824[a]		.679
	.656[a]	.275	.704
Detroit	.628[a]		.394
	.305[a]	.530[a]	.565
Kansas City	.652[a]		.425
	.247	.867[a]	.857
Los Angeles	.727[a]		.529
	.782[a]	.792[a]	.824
Memphis	.806[a]		.650
	.916[a]	.808[a]	.878
Milwaukee	.943[a]		.889
	.750[a]	.252	.896
Philadelphia	.566[a]		.320
	.252[a]	.793[a]	.748
Richmond	.657[a]		.432
	.682[a]	.704[a]	.714
St. Louis	.630[a]		.397
	.426[a]	.739[a]	.726
Shreveport	.799[a]		.638
	.903[a]	.708[a]	.820
Tampa-St. Petersburg	.238		.566
	.415	.801[a]	.661

[a]Significant at 0.01 level. [b]Significant at 0.05 level.

[c]Simple correlation on first line and partial correlations on second line for each city.

related to FAMINC but are positive functions of DISCBD. Therefore housing variables will be included in the next analysis.

Such housing variables probably include median value of owner occupied units (VALOWN), median rent of renter occupied units (MDRENT), and per cent sound occupied units (PCSOND), which are positively related to FAMINC. At the same time MDRENT and PCSOND are positively related to DISCBD. Since WIV/HD has also been shown to be related to per cent owner occupied units (PCONOC), PCONOC will be included in the analysis. However, FAMINC will not be used since I want to examine the relationship between WIV/HD and housing regardless of variation in FAMINC. I hypothesize that the above housing variables, VALOWN, MDRENT, PCSOND, and PCONOC plus DISCBD will predict most of the variation in WIV/HD. Furthermore, the prediction is that the relationship between WIV/HD and DISCBD holding the housing variables constant will be insignificant. The model employed is

$$\begin{aligned} WIV/HD = a + b(PCONOC) + c(PCSOND) + d\,(VALOWN) + \\ e(MDRENT) + f(DISCBD) \end{aligned} \qquad (23)$$

The results of the analysis of model 23 are contained in Table 35.

The r^2 for each city indicates that model 23 is a good predictor of WIV/HD. The lowest r^2 was Tampa-St. Petersburg with an r^2 of 0.799. Thus the spatial variation of black families with both husband and wife present appears to be a function of the spatial variation in housing characteristics among black residential areas in a city. The regression coefficients of DISCBD are significant at least at the 0.10 level in only eight cities. Therefore the previous suggestion that the spatial variation of WIV/HD is related to the spatial variation in housing variables with respect to the CBD seems to be supported in part. However, other housing characteristics or non-housing factors not included in the analysis must still be affecting the spatial variation in WIV/HD.

Interestingly, fourteen of the regression coefficients of PCONOC are significant even when the other variables are held constant. This indicates that variation in WIV/HD and PCONOC is closely related among black residential areas. This may follow from a strong tendency for families with husband and wife present to own their homes. The positive coefficients for PCSOND suggest that higher WIV/HD is found in residential areas with good quality housing. This may reflect either the effect of income or a greater desire on the part of black households with husband and wife present compared with other types of households to live in residential areas with good quality housing. The coefficients of VALOWN were generally not significantly different from zero. However, the coefficients of MDRENT are positive and significant at the 0.10 level in twelve cities.

Since the income of a household determines, in part, the type of housing the family can purchase and residential areas vary in terms of FAMINC, this variable will be added

TABLE 35

RELATION OF PER CENT HOUSEHOLDS WHICH ARE HUSBAND-WIFE HOUSEHOLDS (WIV/HD) TO HOUSING VARIABLES AND DISTANCE FROM THE CBD (DISCBD)

City	Independent Variables[d]					r^2
	PCONOC	PCSOND	VALOWN	MDRENT	DISCBD	
Atlanta	.2287[a] (.0576)	.0576[c] (.0309)	-.000009[b] (.000004)	.00407[a] (.00090)	.0493[b] (.0191)	.853
Baltimore	.2577[a] (.0496)	.1033[a] (.0338)	.000000 (.000004)	.00303[a] (.00064)	-.0103 (.0168)	.864
Birmingham	.0845[b] (.0323)	.2327[a] (.0428)	-.000019[a] (.000006)	.00386[a] (.00136)	.0471[a] (.0146)	.803
Cincinnati	.3475[a] (.1056)	-.0337 (.0506)	.000004 (.000007)	.00288[c] (.00164)	.0504 (.0399)	.907
Columbia	.4000[a] (.1024)	.0471 (.0661)	.000008 (.000013)	.00301 (.00221)	.0317 (.0225)	.918
Columbus	.1707 (.1568)	.1789[c] (.0918)	-.000015 (.000009)	.00344[b] (.00151)	.1671 (.1367)	.854
Detroit	.3555[a] (.0286)	.0547[b] (.0217)	-.000007[a] (.000002)	.00279[a] (.00050)	.0048 (.0110)	.849
Kansas City	.4124[a] (.0559)	.0845 (.0839)	.000015 (.000010)	.00335[c] (.00167)	-.0175 (.0491)	.954
Los Angeles	.3494[a] (.0450)	-.0069 (.0394)	-.000002 (.000003)	.00384[a] (.00114)	.0695[a] (.0155)	.875
Memphis	.1282[a] (.0388)	.0990[a] (.0360)	.000001 (.000006)	.00170[c] (.00089)	.1238[a] (.0161)	.870
Milwaukee	-.1141 (.1871)	.0372 (.0595)	-.000004 (.000007)	.00287 (.00165)	.3539[b] (.1194)	.913
Philadelphia	.2564[a] (.0393)	.1554[a] (.0348)	.000003 (.000004)	.00160[c] (.00083)	.0308[a] (.0096)	.836
Richmond	.2699[a] (.0848)	.2353[a] (.0707)	-.000006 (.000009)	.00191 (.00126)	.0601 (.0384)	.873
St. Louis	.2640[a] (.0461)	.1033[b] (.0384)	-.000015[a] (.000003)	.00503[a] (.00083)	.0308[c] (.0154)	.923
Shreveport	.1295[b] (.0560)	.1765[b] (.0800)	-.000019[c] (.000010)	-.00181 (.00169)	.0511[c] (.0258)	.847
Tampa-St. Petersburg	.2369[a] (.0714)	.0166 (.0504)	-.000003 (.000009)	.00231[b] (.00094)	.0082 (.0132)	.799

[a]Regression coefficient significant at 0.01 level.

[b]Regression coefficient significant at 0.05 level.

[c]Regression coefficient significant at 0.10 level.

[d]Standard errors of regression coefficients are enclosed in parentheses.

to model 23. The results of the analysis are contained in Table 36.

The addition of FAMINC to model 23 did not substantially increase the prediction of WIV/HD. The largest increase in r^2 was in Columbus with Δr^2 of only 4.6 per cent. In fact, the only variable which shows a significant change in importance in the regression equation was MDRENT. The regression coefficient of MDRENT is significant in seven cities in Table 36 whereas when FAMINC was not included the coefficient of MDRENT was significant in twelve cities. The reason for this decline in significance is probably because FAMINC and MDRENT are so highly correlated in most cities. The implication of the continuing significance of PCSOND when FAMINC is added to the regression equation is that black households with both husband and wife present have a greater desire to live in residential areas with good quality housing than other types of households, apart from the effect of income. The small change in the significant regression coefficients of DISCBD can be interpreted to mean that the spatial variation in WIV/HD with respect to the CBD cannot be accounted for by factors related to income. Perhaps the increase in WIV/HD with an increase in DISCBD results from preferences by black households with both husband and wife present for "suburban" living apart from any preferences with regards to housing characteristics. Finally the continued importance of PCONOC even when FAMINC is held constant supports the contention of Frazier that black residential areas are differentiated such that higher proportions of families with both husband and wife present are associated with higher rates of owner occupancy.

Extended and Augmented Families and Housing

The living arrangements of households are certainly affected by the presence of relatives or nonrelatives in the dwelling unit. If relatives or nonrelatives are not part of the household when the residential location decision is made, the addition of these members after the household moves may strain the resources of the household and lead to crowding in the dwelling unit. However, if relatives and nonrelatives are part of the household when it moves, their presence can be taken into account in the residential decision. In this study, however, the time when relatives or nonrelatives are added to the households cannot be distinguished. In spite of this limitation the analysis of the spatial variation in relatives and nonrelatives among black residential areas can be approached by relating the characteristics of families and their housing to the decision to take relatives and nonrelatives into the household. Following Billingsley's discussion of black families, families with relatives living with them will be called _extended families_ and families with nonrelatives present will be called _augmented families_.[1]

---

[1] Andrew Billingsley, _Black Families in White America_ (Englewood Cliffs, N.J.: Prentice-Hall, Inc., 1968), pp. 19-21.

TABLE 36

ADDITION OF MEDIAN FAMILY INCOME (FAMINC) TO MODEL 23

City	Independent Variables						Δr^2 [d]
	FAMINC	PCONOC	PCSOND	VALOWN	MDRENT	DISCBD	
Atlanta	.000053[b] (.000021)	.1241[c] (.0682)	.0419 (.0295)	-.000011[a] (.000004)	.00286[a] (.00097)	.0531[a] (.0179)	.023
Baltimore	.000027 (.000017)	.1929[a] (.0638)	.0955[a] (.0338)	-.000004 (.000005)	.00245[a] (.00073)	-.0046 (.0170)	.006
Birmingham	.000022 (.000015)	.0629[c] (.0351)	.2126[a] (.0444)	-.000020[a] (.000006)	.00266[c] (.00157)	.0436[a] (.0146)	.010
Cincinnati	.000038 (.000040)	.2391 (.1561)	.0101 (.0688)	.000001 (.000008)	.00081 (.00274)	.0726 (.0464)	.004
Columbia	-.000006 (.000060)	.4117[c] (.1610)	.0449 (.0757)	.000009 (.000015)	.00319 (.00301)	.0310 (.0258)	.000
Columbus	-.000135[c] (.000066)	.1189 (.1391)	.1553[c] (.0809)	-.000015 (.000008)	.00992[b] (.00345)	.4698[b] (.1906)	.046
Detroit	-.000009 (.000009)	.3726[a] (.0335)	.0609[a] (.0226)	-.000006[a] (.000002)	.00310[a] (.00059)	.0062 (.0111)	.001
Kansas City	.000002 (.000028)	.4090[a] (.0839)	.0855 (.0880)	.000015 (.000013)	.00329 (.00206)	-.0162 (.0550)	.000
Los Angeles	.000050[a] (.000010)	.2590[a] (.0435)	-.0142 (.0347)	-.000007[b] (.000003)	.00153 (.00110)	.0888[a] (.0141)	.030
Memphis	.000063[a] (.000020)	.0252 (.0480)	.0813[b] (.0329)	-.000002 (.000006)	-.00007 (.00098)	.1324[a] (.0148)	.028
Milwaukee	-.000001 (.000028)	-.1126 (.2057)	.0372 (.0622)	-.000004 (.000007)	.00290 (.00222)	.3545[b] (.1278)	.000
Philadelphia	.000018 (.000013)	.2182[a] (.0484)	.1458[a] (.0354)	.000001 (.000004)	.00107 (.00092)	.0299[a] (.0096)	.002
Richmond	.000006 (.000024)	.2531[b] (.1100)	.2326[a] (.0735)	-.000007 (.000010)	.00160 (.00177)	.0640 (.0424)	.000
St. Louis	.000017 (.000013)	.2179[a] (.0566)	.0964[b] (.0383)	-.000016[a] (.000003)	.00442[a] (.00093)	.0323[b] (.0152)	.003
Shreveport	.000085[b] (.000035)	.0262 (.0656)	.1298[c] (.0735)	-.000018[c] (.000009)	-.00348[b] (.00165)	.0657[b] (.0237)	.039
Tampa-St. Petersburg	.000059 (.000055)	.1801[c] (.0885)	.0469 (.0575)	-.000003 (.000009)	.00102 (.00152)	.0082 (.0132)	.015

[a]Significant at 0.01 level.

[b]Significant at 0.05 level.

[c]Significant at 0.10 level.

[d]Increase in r^2 with addition of FAMINC to model 23.

Extended families

Extended families can develop for several reasons. Deaths in a household may necessitate the surviving members moving in with relatives. The dissolution of a marriage may mean that the mother and children move in with grandparents or vice versa. A household may experience financial difficulties and have to move in with relatives. Finally, relatives may live in a household irrespective of any "difficulties" because this is considered desirable. Because the addition of relatives to a household puts an added strain on financial resources family income may be a factor in the formation of extended families, although the exact form of this relationship is not clear. On the one hand the higher the income of the family the greater the capability of supporting relatives. Yet the higher the income of the family the less likely the family will have relatives who need to be supported in the household. Therefore, median family income (FAMINC) will be controlled in the analysis of black residential areas. The reason is that FAMINC is positively related to housing characteristics of residential areas such as per cent owner occupied units (PCONOC), median number of rooms (MROOMS), and median value of owner occupied units (VALOWN), which were discussed in the previous chapter. Also several of the above housing characteristics are related to distance from the CBD (DISCBD). Since the extended family is almost by definition larger than nuclear families (husband, wife, and their children) the extended families will need more space than the nuclear family. Therefore spatial variation in MROOMS may be an important determinant of spatial variation in extended families.

This greater demand for space can probably be best met in owner occupied dwellings. Furthermore the inclusion of relatives in a household requires greater resources which are in turn needed for purchasing a dwelling. Therefore it is anticipated that spatial variation in PCONOC may be a determinant of spatial variation in extended families. Since PCONOC may be positively related to variation in extended families, median value of owner occupied units (VALOWN) will be used rather than median rent of renter occupied units (MDRENT). The ratio of the number of other relatives of heads of households divided by the number of heads of households in a residential area (OTR/HD) will be employed as a measure of extended families. The higher the ratio the greater the incidence of extended families in a black residential area. Thus to examine the determinants of spatial variation in OTR/HD I hypothesize the following regression model.

$$\text{OTR/HD} = a + b(\text{FAMINC}) + c(\text{PCONOC}) + d(\text{MROOMS}) + e(\text{VALOWN}) + f(\text{DISCBD}) \qquad (24)$$

The results of the analysis of model 24 contained in Table 37 indicate that the model is not an especially good predictor of OTR/HD. Most of the r^2 values are in the neighborhood of 0.500. The hypothesis that MROOMS is an important determinant of

TABLE 37

DETERMINANTS OF RATIO OF OTHER RELATIVES OF HEADS OF HOUSEHOLDS TO HEADS OF HOUSEHOLDS (OTR/HD)

City	Independent Variables[d]					r^2
	FAMINC	PCONOC	MROOMS	VALOWN	DISCBD	
Atlanta	-.000032 (.000067)	.6050[a] (.2831)	-.0836 (.0769)	-.000029[c] (.000016)	-.0298 (.0643)	.270
Baltimore	-.000018 (.000055)	-.2931 (.2640)	.2225[a] (.0524)	-.000039[b] (.000017)	.1694[b] (.0645)	.433
Birmingham	.000070[b] (.000028)	.2303 (.1495)	.0114 (.0550)	-.000034[b] (.000015)	-.0140 (.0314)	.584
Cincinnati	.000017 (.000043)	.2669 (.3699)	.0556 (.0936)	.000001 (.000015)	.0036 (.0816)	.661
Columbia	-.000372 (.000213)	2.0968[b] (.8564)	-.4397 (.2598)	.000039 (.000066)	.1064 (.1097)	.803
Columbus	-.000043 (.000076)	-.1250 (.2972)	.1729[c] (.0797)	-.000011 (.000016)	-.2367 (.2359)	.570
Detroit	-.000058[a] (.000017)	.1235[c] (.0744)	.1684[a] (.0157)	-.000001 (.000005)	-.0023 (.0251)	.569
Kansas City	.000022 (.000045)	-.2275 (.1668)	.1809[a] (.0465)	-.000014 (.000020)	-.1671[c] (.0826)	.721
Los Angeles	-.000033[c] (.000017)	.1422 (.1043)	.0661[b] (.0301)	-.000001 (.000005)	-.0567[b] (.0245)	.226
Memphis	-.000009 (.000046)	.1983 (.1656)	.0233 (.0637)	-.000031[c] (.000017)	.0927[c] (.0515)	.570
Milwaukee	.000032 (.000059)	.3059 (.5019)	.4729[b] (.2148)	.000014 (.000017)	-.5594[c] (.2978)	.554
Philadelphia	-.000050[b] (.000024)	.0609 (.1203)	.1138[a] (.0216)	-.000034[a] (.000009)	.0261 (.0198)	.508
Richmond	.000090 (.000066)	-.5193 (.3982)	.1176 (.1038)	-.000080[a] (.000026)	.3102[c] (.1556)	.548
St. Louis	-.000021 (.000032)	-.3074 (.1853)	.1260[b] (.0471)	.000010 (.000009)	.1203[b] (.0462)	.435
Shreveport	.000013 (.000073)	-.1099 (.2302)	.0560 (.1181)	-.000019 (.000018)	.0902[c] (.0508)	.648
Tampa-St. Petersburg	.000158[b] (.000063)	-.0603 (.1855)	.0025 (.0624)	-.000024[c] (.000011)	.0083 (.0249)	.599

[a]Regression coefficient significant at 0.01 level.

[b]Regression coefficient significant at 0.05 level.

[c]Regression coefficient significant at 0.10 level.

[d]Standard errors of regression coefficients are enclosed in parentheses.

OTR/HD is partially confirmed. The regression coefficients of MROOMS are significant at the 0.10 level in eight cities. This suggests that higher proportions of relatives of the heads of households are found in residential areas with large dwelling units even when other housing characteristics, especially VALOWN, are held constant. PCONOC does not appear to be an important determinant of OTR/HD. The coefficients of PCONOC were significant at the 0.10 level in only three cities. The negative coefficients of VALOWN suggest that high ratios of OTR/HD are found in residential areas with low-valued owner occupied dwellings. Since PCONOC was held constant this may mean that black households in low-valued owner occupied dwellings are more likely to take in relatives than black households in high-valued owner occupied dwellings. Alternatively, households with relatives present who prefer to own may be more likely to move into low-valued dwellings than are households without relatives present who also prefer to own. This may result from the lower income households tending to have more relatives present than higher income households. The spatial location of households with relatives with respect to the CBD does not appear to follow any pattern in the sixteen cities.

Because of the poor prediction of OTR/HD in model 24 several variables will be added to the regression equation. The first variable added is per cent sound housing (PCSOND). Extended families may be overcrowded which could lead to deterioration in the dwellings. Hence PCSOND may be inversely related to OTR/HD. Per cent single family dwellings (PCSFDW) is added as a measure of dwelling type. Median rent of renter occupied units (MDRENT) is added because it is a more sensitive indicator of variation in dwelling price among residential areas than is VALOWN. The analysis of the revised model is contained in Table 38.

The Δr^2 values indicate that the additional variables substantially increased the predictability of OTR/HD. The largest increase in r^2 was recorded in Atlanta with Δr^2 of .495. The r^2 values in Table 38 are high enough to suggest that the revised model has captured some of the important variation in OTR/HD. MROOMS remains a significant predictor of variation in OTR/HD. Ten of the regression coefficients of MROOMS are significant at the 0.10 level. This is two more than in model 24. Hence it can be concluded that high proportions of extended families are found in black residential areas with large dwelling units and low proportions of extended families are found in residential areas with small dwelling units holding other factors in the model constant. The other variable which contributes significantly to the prediction of OTR/HD is PCSOND. Seven coefficients are negative and significant at the 0.10 level and altogether eleven coefficients are negative and larger than their standard errors. This means that the proportion of extended families and housing quality in black residential areas are inversely related. Perhaps the extended family must sacrifice on quality of housing to obtain the large housing which the family needs.

Augmented families

The augmented family is probably a characteristic of lower income black families rather than upper income. An augmented family may arise because a friend of the family needs a place to live and does not have enough money to live alone. Another reason for the existence of augmented families may be that the family needs extra money, perhaps to pay for its housing, and therefore takes in boarders.[1]

Assuming that augmented families are more prevalent in lower income black families than in higher income black families, one would expect that augmented families live in housing which is rented, has small number of rooms, is low rent, and is close to the CBD. Given the spatial differentiation of housing among residential areas, I hypothesize that the above housing characteristics are important determinants of the spatial variation in augmented families. The measure of augmented families in a residential area which will be used is the ratio of nonrelatives of heads of households to heads of households (NRL/HD) The higher NRL/HD the greater the incidence of augmented families in a residential area. The following regression model forms the basis of the analysis.

$$NRL/HD = a + b(FAMINC) + c(PCONOC) + d(MROOMS) + e(MDRENT) + f(DISCBD) \quad (25)$$

From the results of the analysis in Table 39 I conclude that model 25 does not provide a good prediction of variation in NRL/HD. Most of the regression coefficients are not significant at the 0.10 level. The only significant pattern is the fact that nine of the ten regression coefficients for DISCBD which are larger than their standard errors are negative. This suggests that high rates of augmented families are found close to the CBD and low rates are found farther from the CBD. This pattern was hypothesized based on a rationale that the tendency to take in nonrelatives was inversely related to family income. These families are likely to live close to the CBD for reasons discussed in the previous chapter. However, since FAMINC as well as other variables were held constant in the model, the implication of the result of an inverse relation between NRL/HD and DISCBD is that there are other factors besides those variables included in the model which account for the spatial location of augmented families with respect to the CBD.

Since model 25 did not provide satisfactory prediction of NRL/HD several housing variables will be added. It has been suggested that family income is inversely related to tendency to take in nonrelatives. Since the quality of dwelling which a family occupies is probably positively related to its income I hypothesize that NRL/HD is negatively related

---

[1]Drake and Cayton provide a vivid picture of lower and middle class black family life in Chicago during the Depression of the 1930's. The families in these classes had to take in boarders to supplement their income. See Drake and Cayton, Black Metropolis, pp. 576, 664.

TABLE 38

ADDITIONAL DETERMINANTS OF RATIO OF OTHER RELATIVES OF HEADS OF HOUSEHOLDS TO HEADS OF HOUSEHOLDS (OTR/HD)

City	Independent Variables								r^2	Δr^{2} [d]
	FAMINC	PCONOC	PCSOND	MROOMS	PCSFDW	VALOWN	MDRENT	DISCBD		
Atlanta	-.000148[a] (.000049)	-.1158 (.2191)	-.5946[a] (.0966)	.2154[a] (.0659)	.0422 (.1139)	-.000028[a] (.000010)	.01356[a] (.00216)	.0197 (.0411)	.765	.495
Baltimore	-.000055 (.000058)	-.1092 (.2535)	-.2350[b] (.1168)	.2258[a] (.0615)	-.2789[c] (.1525)	-.000050[a] (.000018)	.00493[c] (.00270)	.2119[a] (.0673)	.533	.100
Birmingham	.000044 (.000032)	.2215 (.1322)	-.2668[b] (.1003)	.0242 (.0505)	.3141[b] (.1170)	-.000023[c] (.000013)	-.00851[b] (.00340)	-.0059 (.0353)	.727	.143
Cincinnati	.000038 (.000086)	.2374 (.4042)	.0920 (.1814)	.0311 (.1302)	-.0632 (.1958)	-.000004 (.000018)	-.00050 (.00616)	.0214 (.1123)	.671	.010
Columbia	-.000109 (.000286)	.8310 (1.4011)	-1.0278 (.9981)	.4498 (.7247)	-.4147 (.9218)	.000058 (.000068)	.00130 (.02201)	-.0222 (.1718)	.900	.097
Columbus	-.000041 (.000169)	-.3811 (.7577)	-.2851 (.1750)	.2112[b] (.0883)	.1657 (.4905)	.000012 (.000022)	-.00210 (.00937)	-.0370 (.3993)	.700	.130
Detroit	-.000025 (.000020)	-.1803 (.1112)	-.0782 (.0482)	.1647[a] (.0169)	.2466[a] (.0721)	.000002 (.000005)	-.00049 (.00140)	-.0008 (.0240)	.618	.049
Kansas City	.000007 (.000053)	-.4112 (.2594)	.0343 (.1686)	.1782[a] (.0540)	.1545 (.1407)	-.000014 (.000025)	.00195 (.00424)	-.1494 (.1108)	.742	.021
Los Angeles	-.000040[b] (.000018)	.0442 (.1172)	-.1698[b] (.0645)	.0768[a] (.0288)	.0632 (.0731)	.000003 (.000005)	.00336[c] (.00191)	-.0582[b] (.0252)	.330	.104
Memphis	-.000090[c] (.000047)	.1175 (.1470)	-.4873[a] (.0889)	.1899[a] (.0537)	-.0076 (.1034)	-.000009 (.000014)	.01232[a] (.00235)	.0674[c] (.0378)	.798	.228

Milwaukee	-.000033	.2925	-.0853	.2240	.0315	.000017	.00934	-.4285	.674	.120
	(.000069)	(.5155)	(.1504)	(.2643)	(.2263)	(.000020)	(.00657)	(.3282)		
Philadelphia	-.000039	.0545	-.2644[a]	.1362[a]	.0029	-.000030[a]	.00151	.0070	.588	.080
	(.000024)	(.1079)	(.0697)	(.0219)	(.0680)	(.000009)	(.00176)	(.0181)		
Richmond	-.000019	-.2724	-.6939[a]	.1453[b]	.1149	.000004	.00993[b]	.3282[a]	.887	.339
	(.000049)	(.3096)	(.1888)	(.0649)	(.1781)	(.000020)	(.00408)	(.0874)		
St. Louis	.000006	-.1144	-.1952	.2168[a]	-.2536[b]	.000013	-.00384	.1122[b]	.540	.105
	(.000037)	(.2295)	(.1188)	(.0575)	(.1162)	(.000010)	(.00298)	(.0438)		
Shreveport	.000006	-.0923	.0732	.0312	.0570	-.000023	-.00015	.0932	.651	.003
	(.000095)	(.2714)	(.2384)	(.1577)	(.2695)	(.000024)	(.00478)	(.0718)		
Tampa-St. Petersburg	.000168	-.1501	.0988	-.0075	.0367	-.000035[c]	.00036	e	.621	.022
	(.000117)	(.2551)	(.1164)	(.0685)	(.1756)	(.000016)	(.00317)			

[a]Significant at 0.01 level.

[b]Significant at 0.05 level.

[c]Significant at 0.10 level.

[d]Increase in r^2 above model 24.

[e]Variable deleted from regression because contribution to total variance was too small.

TABLE 39

DETERMINANTS OF RATIO OF NONRELATIVES OF HEADS OF HOUSEHOLDS TO HEADS OF HOUSEHOLDS (NRL/HD)

City	Independent Variables[d]					r^2
	FAMINC	PCONOC	MROOMS	MDRENT	DISCBD	
Atlanta	-.000031 (.000026)	.0831 (.0959)	-.0265 (.0249)	.00260[b] (.00121)	-.0277 (.0191)	.284
Baltimore	-.000016 (.000014)	-.1529[c] (.0770)	.0540[a] (.0156)	.00046 (.00083)	-.0089 (.0183)	.329
Birmingham	-.000013 (.000012)	-.0228 (.0420)	-.0100 (.0162)	-.00084 (.00118)	-.0436[a] (.0102)	.608
Cincinnati	.000037[c] (.000018)	-.0707 (.0833)	-.0147 (.0198)	-.00047 (.00134)	.0227 (.0270)	.466
Columbia	.000080 (.000046)	-.2107 (.1530)	-.0442 (.0497)	-.00369[c] (.00183)	-.0194 (.0199)	.883
Columbus	.000087 (.000083)	.0492 (.1746)	.0193 (.0427)	-.00541 (.00422)	-.4135[c] (.2105)	.535
Detroit	-.000008 (.000009)	-.0711[c] (.0399)	.0447[a] (.0096)	-.00084 (.00083)	-.0263[c] (.0147)	.279
Kansas City	-.000018 (.000016)	-.0609 (.0674)	.0510[b] (.0213)	-.00108 (.00145)	-.0409 (.0270)	.340
Los Angeles	-.000011 (.000008)	-.0739 (.0515)	.0258[c] (.0145)	.00278[a] (.00094)	-.0796[a] (.0124)	.450
Memphis	-.000040[c] (.000020)	.0873 (.0526)	-.0135 (.0194)	.00227[b] (.00090)	-.0561[a] (.0140)	.531
Milwaukee	.000045 (.000028)	.6127[a] (.1990)	.0883 (.1040)	-.00120 (.00247)	-.5188[a] (.1123)	.669
Philadelphia	-.000032[b] (.000012)	-.0546 (.0619)	.0313[a] (.0108)	.00154 (.00095)	-.0087 (.0098)	.145
Richmond	-.000029 (.000025)	-.0299 (.1415)	-.0124 (.0363)	.00622[a] (.00212)	-.0816 (.0543)	.448
St. Louis	.000002 (.000015)	-.1771[b] (.0733)	-.0063 (.0219)	.00005 (.00105)	.0419[b] (.0180)	.295
Shreveport	.000013 (.000036)	-.0705 (.0999)	-.0147 (.0522)	.00145 (.00175)	-.0162 (.0274)	.664
Tampa-St. Petersburg	.000206[b] (.000076)	-.4030[b] (.1589)	.0353 (.0551)	-.00123 (.00204)	.0094 (.0213)	.440

[a]Regression coefficient significant at 0.01 level.

[b]Regression coefficient significant at 0.05 level.

[c]Regression coefficient significant at 0.10 level.

[d]Standard errors of regression coefficients are enclosed in parentheses.

to per cent sound quality housing (PCSOND), given variation in housing quality among residential areas. Per cent single family dwellings (PCSFDW) will be used as a measure of housing type. Since an assumption is that augmented families tend to have low income which means in turn that the dwelling is probably rented and an apartment, then NRL/HD would be negatively related to PCSFDW. Median value of owner occupied units (VALOWN) is employed as an additional measure of variation in dwelling cost among residential areas. The analysis of the expanded model is contained in Table 40.

Judging from the Δr^2, the expanded model provides substantially better prediction of NRL/HD than does model 25. The most important independent predictor of NRL/HD is PCSOND with twelve coefficients significant at the 0.10 level. The negative sign of these coefficients means that NRL/HD is inversely related to PCSOND, which supports the hypothesis. Only six of the coefficients of MROOMS are positive and significant at the 0.10 level. However, fourteen of the coefficients are positive and nine of these are larger than their standard errors. Thus, there is some meager evidence for concluding that NRL/HD is positively associated with MROOMS holding other variables in the model constant. The only other variable which seems to contribute significantly to variation in NRL/HD is DISCBD. Twelve of the sixteen coefficients are negative. Of these twelve, nine are larger than their standard errors and five of the nine are significant at the 0.10 level. Although the evidence is very tentative, augmented black families seem to live in residential areas relatively close to the CBD. Perhaps the reason for this pattern is that the poorest families who might wish to take in lodgers live close to the CBD. At the same time single men or women who are potential lodgers also may live in these same residential areas in boarding houses and hotels. Given a demand and supply in the same residential areas, the formation of augmented families is the result.[1] However, low income per se may not lead to the formation of augmented families. Rather, an additional factor may also be necessary. Only particular types of low income households may take in boarders. These households may include the families with only older children or no children. Low income families with young children might be less likely to take in nonrelatives since they would not want to take chances with the potential negative influence of boarders on the young children.

Conclusions

The evidence presented seems to imply that the incidence of extended and augmented families in residential areas is negatively associated with quality of housing and positively

---

[1]Because the data are aggregated by census tracts, the exact form of the individual household patterns must remain purely speculative.

TABLE 40

ADDITIONAL DETERMINANTS OF RATIO OF NONRELATIVES OF HEADS OF HOUSEHOLDS TO HEADS OF HOUSEHOLDS (NRL/HD)

City	Independent Variables								r^2	$\Delta r^{2\,d}$
	FAMINC	PCONOC	PCSOND	MROOMS	PCSFDW	VALOWN	MDRENT	DISCBD		
Atlanta	-.000036 (.000024)	-.1648 (.1074)	-.1532[a] (.0473)	.0606[c] (.0323)	.0786 (.0559)	.000003 (.000005)	.00331[a] (.00106)	-.0333 (.0202)	.515	.231
Baltimore	-.000001 (.000015)	-.0871 (.0674)	-.1464[a] (.0310)	.0518[a] (.0164)	-.0438 (.0405)	-.000004 (.000005)	.00056 (.00072)	.0063 (.0179)	.537	.208
Birmingham	-.000010 (.000010)	.0289 (.0422)	-.0689[b] (.0320)	-.0205 (.0161)	.0281 (.0373)	.000017[a] (.000004)	-.00040 (.00109)	-.0276[b] (.0112)	.737	.129
Cincinnati	.000018 (.000024)	-.0233 (.1138)	-.0685 (.0511)	.0111 (.0367)	-.0411 (.0551)	.000002 (.000005)	.00029 (.00173)	.0166 (.0316)	.534	.068
Columbia	.000095[c] (.000035)	-.5398[b] (.1696)	-.0841 (.1208)	.1011 (.0878)	.1926 (.1116)	-.000002 (.000008)	-.00440 (.00267)	-.0590[c] (.0208)	.967	.084
Columbus	.000126 (.000079)	-.4794 (.3529)	-.1922[c] (.0815)	.0498 (.0411)	.3514 (.2285)	.000018 (.000010)	-.00869[c] (.00437)	-.2260 (.1860)	.803	.268
Detroit	.000003 (.000012)	-.0945 (.0653)	-.1125[a] (.0283)	.0392[a] (.0099)	.0184 (.0423)	.000003 (.000003)	-.00029 (.00082)	-.0212 (.0141)	.359	.080
Kansas City	-.000010 (.000022)	-.0353 (.1060)	.0729 (.0689)	.0490[b] (.0221)	-.0423 (.0575)	-.000005 (.000010)	-.00195 (.00173)	-.0445 (.0453)	.410	.070
Los Angeles	-.000020[b] (.000008)	-.0482 (.0551)	-.0717[b] (.0303)	.0244[c] (.0135)	.0241 (.0344)	.000009[a] (.000002)	.00248[a] (.00090)	-.0688[a] (.0119)	.548	.098
Memphis	-.000039[b] (.000019)	.0720 (.0589)	-.1191[a] (.0356)	.0198 (.0215)	-.0226 (.0414)	.000006 (.000005)	.00383[a] (.00094)	-.0597[a] (.0151)	.650	.119

Milwaukee	.000043[c] (.000022)	.7467[a] (.1620)	-.1343[b] (.0473)	.0615 (.0830)	-.1221 (.0711)	-.000006 (.000006)	-.00209 (.00207)	-.3698[a] (.1031)	.848	.179
Philadelphia	-.000016 (.000012)	-.0158 (.0556)	-.1396[a] (.0359)	.0461[a] (.0113)	-.0663[c] (.0350)	-.000008[c] (.000005)	.00149 (.00091)	-.0091 (.0093)	.280	.135
Richmond	.000007 (.000024)	-.2237 (.1509)	-.1617[c] (.0920)	.0249 (.0316)	.1217 (.0868)	.000004 (.000010)	.00394[c] (.00199)	-.0672 (.0426)	.729	.281
St. Louis	-.000006 (.000013)	-.1068 (.0815)	-.1006[b] (.0422)	.0201 (.0204)	.0152 (.0413)	.000014[a] (.000003)	-.00063 (.00106)	.0214 (.0156)	.554	.259
Shreveport	.000005 (.000038)	-.0525 (.1076)	-.0454 (.0946)	-.0109 (.0625)	.0459 (.1069)	.000017[c] (.000009)	.00160 (.00190)	-.0115 (.0285)	.738	.074
Tampa-St. Petersburg	.000060 (.000085)	-.3050 (.1864)	-.2282[b] (.0915)	.0697 (.0502)	.0218 (.1336)	.000007 (.000013)	.00231 (.00233)	.0198 (.0211)	.666	.226

[a]Significant at 0.01 level.

[b]Significant at 0.05 level.

[c]Significant at 0.10 level.

[d]Increase in r^2 above model 25.

associated with dwelling size, holding other factors constant. It is difficult to isolate whether extended and augmented families live in poor quality housing because of their low resources or whether housing in residential areas with large numbers of extended and augmented families deteriorates because these families are too large for the housing facilities. I tend to favor the first reason. Black families with low resources are more likely to live in poor quality housing and take in relatives or nonrelatives.

The finding that the incidence of extended and augmented families in a residential area is positively related to MROOMS may result from the space demands of these households. These families could obtain large housing by sacrificing on quality of housing.

Finally, the moderate size of the r^2 for even the expanded models with OTR/HD and NRL/HD as dependent variables may result from at least two causes. First, the relationship between extended and augmented family characteristics and residential choice is not clear. Hence the deductions with regards to residential areas may be grossly in error. Secondly, extended and augmented families may be such a common occurrence among black households that little differentiation by residential areas results.

CHAPTER VI

RELATIONS BETWEEN INCOME AND FAMILY TYPE CHARACTERISTICS

So far the relationship between family income and housing and between selected family characteristics and housing has been examined. However, the relationship between family income and family characteristics has not been explicitly considered; although in the last chapter median family income (FAMINC) was frequently included in the analyses since it was suspected that variations in FAMINC might be related to variations in family characteristics among black residential areas. Now the relationship between FAMINC and the family characteristic variables will be analyzed. As an approach to the analysis, findings in a body of literature variously known as social area analysis or factorial ecology[1] will be evaluated since this literature contains a development of some ideas about the relationship between socioeconomic status and family characteristics among residential areas within cities.

Findings of Social Area Analyses and Factorial Ecologies

A general conclusion to be found in the literature of social area analysis and factorial ecology is that there are at least two fundamental and relatively independent (that is, statistically uncorrelated) dimensions to the differentiation of residential areas within cities of "western" culture, socioeconomic status and family status, with ethnic status occurring as a third separate dimension in some cities.[2] Before discussing the implications of this general conclusion for my study of black residential areas, exceptions to the general pattern noted in several American cities will be examined. Van Arsdol, Camilleri,

---

[1] A clarification of the social area analysis or factorial ecology terminology is contained in Brian J. L. Berry and Philip H. Rees, "The Factorial Ecology of Calcutta," American Journal of Sociology, LXXIV (March, 1969), 454-59.

[2] Janet L. Abu-Lughod, "Testing the Theory of Social Area Analysis: The Ecology of Cairo, Egypt," American Sociological Review, XXXIV (April, 1969), 198-212; and Robert A. Murdie, Factorial Ecology of Metropolitan Toronto, 1951-1961, Department of Geography Research Paper No. 116 (Chicago: Department of Geography, University of Chicago, 1969), pp. 17-31.

and Schmid have reported that fertility was an important component of the social rank (socioeconomic status) dimension in three southern cities, Atlanta, Birmingham, and Louisville and one border city, Kansas City. However, fertility is usually considered a component of the urbanization (family status) dimension by the social area analysts.[1] The authors suggest that the presence of large proportions of Afro-Americans in the four cities combined with their low socioeconomic status may be the factors behind the lack of dis-association between fertility and social rank. However, this explanation raises more questions than it answers.

A more satisfactory means of interpreting the results of Van Arsdol, Camilleri, and Schmid is suggested in a discussion by Janet Abu-Lughod.[2] Interpreting her comments, I would claim that a necessary and sufficient condition for fertility to be associated with socioeconomic status among residential areas is a situation where blacks have low socioeconomic status and high fertility and whites have high socioeconomic status and low fertility and where whites and blacks are residentially segregated. However, where whites and blacks do not differ significantly in fertility, then even though whites and blacks still differ on socioeconomic status and are residentially segregated, fertility will not be associated with socioeconomic status.

Although Table 41 is for 1960, while the Van Arsdol, Camilleri, and Schmid study was for 1950, the data suggest that the most pronounced difference between the fertility of whites and nonwhites (mainly Afro-Americans) occurs in the South. Outside the South the difference is not very significant on the measure employed. Even though whites and blacks may differ by socioeconomic status and may be residentially segregated outside the South, the small difference between white and black fertility may be a factor in the lack of association between fertility and socioeconomic status noted in non-southern cities. However, within southern cities whites and blacks differ on fertility as well as socioeconomic status. Coupled with residential segregation, the result is a situation where fertility is associated with socioeconomic status.

However, neither the finding that socioeconomic status and fertility are associated in several southern cities and one border city nor the finding that Afro-Americans have higher fertility than whites in the South necessarily imply anything about the relationship between socioeconomic status and fertility among Afro-Americans at the level of the individual household or at the aggregate level of the black residential area. Furthermore, the

---

[1] Maurice D. Van Arsdol, Jr., Santo F. Camilleri, and Calvin F. Schmid, "The Generality of Urban Social Area Indexes," American Sociological Review, XXIII (June, 1958), 277-84.

[2] Abu-Lughod, "Testing the Theory of Social Area Analysis: The Ecology of Cairo, Egypt," pp. 208-9.

TABLE 41

CHILDREN EVER BORN PER 1000 EVER-MARRIED WOMEN, 20-39 YEARS OLD, FOR WHITES AND NONWHITES, BY REGION OF RESIDENCE, WITH URBAN AND RURAL RESIDENCE FOR THE SOUTH: 1960

Area	White	Nonwhite	Ratio of Nonwhite to White
Northeast	2124	2276	1.07
North Central	2355	2627	1.12
West	2309	2520	1.09
South			
Total	2247	3179	1.41
Urban	2104	2805	1.33
Rural Nonfarm	2434	3721	1.53
Rural Farm	2691	4452	1.65

Source: U. S., Bureau of the Census, U. S. Census of Population: 1960, Vol. I: Characteristics of the Population (Washington, D. C.: U. S. Government Printing Office, 1964), Table 249, pp. 681-83.

finding that socioeconomic status and family status are independent dimensions of American cities outside the South does not provide any clues concerning the relationship between socioeconomic status and family status among black residential areas. This is because the studies primarily refer to whites, due to the relatively small proportion of Afro-Americans in the population. Instead clues concerning the relationship between socioeconomic status and family status among black residential areas can best be gathered from a synthesis of ideas on fertility and family patterns among black households.

Fertility and Family Patterns among Black Households

One conclusion from studies of fertility is that fertility is inversely related to socioeconomic status as measured by education of woman and occupation of husband among both whites and nonwhites (mainly Afro-Americans).[1] For income, the variable of interest in this study, the situation for 1960 is slightly more complex. For white women, where the wife is under 25 years, there is a positive relation between income and children ever born while for white women over 30 years there is an inverse relation between income and children ever born. However, among nonwhite women, again mainly Afro-

[1]Clyde V. Kiser, "Fertility Trends and Differentials among Nonwhites in the United States," Milbank Memorial Fund Quarterly, XXXVI (April, 1958), 197; and Clyde V. Kiser, Wilson H. Grabill, and Arthur A. Campbell, Trends and Variations in Fertility in the United States (Cambridge: Harvard University Press, 1968), pp. 151 and 207.

Americans, there is an inverse relation between income and children ever born for wives at all ages.[1]

Income and likelihood of both husband and wife being present may also be positively related among black families. This is implied from several sources. First, the highest proportions of households with husband absent appear among the lower class black families.[2] Secondly, 44.1 per cent of urban nonwhite married females with spouse present are in the labor force.[3] Therefore, given that the highest proportion of female headed households occur in the lower class and a relatively high proportion of working wives occur in families in which both husband and wife are present, then families headed by females would tend to have relatively low income and families with both husband and wife present would tend to have relatively high income. This supposition is partially supported by evidence for 1960 when the median family income of nonwhite families with the wife of head present was $3649 while for nonwhite families headed by females, median family income was only $1742.[4] The fact that families with both husband and wife present have higher incomes than female headed families follows partly because these families frequently have two incomes. This fact occurs regardless of any association between income and tendency for husband and wife to remain married and living together.

The relationship between income and extended families is not clear. In the last chapter it was argued that the higher the income of the family the greater the capability of supporting relatives. Yet, the higher the income of the family the less likely the family will have relatives who need to be supported in the household. The evidence in Table 42 indicates that the ratio of other relatives of heads to heads of families increases with family income. However, when family income is below $6000 the ratio is relatively constant. Only above $6000 does the ratio increase significantly.

The relationship between income and augmented black families would seem to be clearer. Families with low incomes and no young children are probably the most likely to take in lodgers to gain added income. Therefore, as argued in the previous chapter, income and tendency to form augmented families are probably inversely related.

---

[1] Kiser, Grabill, and Campbell, Trends and Variations in Fertility in the United States, pp. 208-11.

[2] Billingsley, Black Families in White America, pp. 124-42; and Frazier, The Negro in the United States, pp. 318-33.

[3] U. S., Bureau of the Census, U. S. Census of Population: 1960, Subject Reports, Employment Status and Work Experience, Final Report PC(2)-6A (Washington, D. C.: U. S. Government Printing Office, 1963), Table 4, p. 31.

[4] U. S., Bureau of the Census, U. S. Census of Population: 1960, Subject Reports, Sources and Structure of Family Income, Final Report PC(2)-4C (Washington, D. C.: U. S. Government Printing Office, 1964), Table 12, p. 148.

TABLE 42

NONWHITE FAMILY INCOME IN 1959 BY RATIO OF OTHER RELATIVES OF HEADS TO HEADS OF FAMILIES FOR URBANIZED AREAS: 1960[a]

Family Income	Ratio of Other Relatives of Heads to Heads of Families
Under $2000	.39
$2000-3999	.41
$4000-5999	.45
$6000-7999	.60
$8000 & over	.94

[a]Calculated from U. S., Bureau of the Census, U. S. Census of Population: 1960, Subject Reports, Persons by Family Characteristics, Final Report PC(2)-4B (Washington, D. C.: U. S. Government Printing Office, 1964), Table 12a, p. 116.

Analysis

Turning from the literature concerning fertility and family patterns among black households to specific evidence on the correspondence between income and family type characteristics among black residential areas, we find that such evidence is meager. Again, Frazier's study of Chicago provides some evidence. In general, he concluded that the character and size of the family group were related to what he called the "general culture" in the different zones in Chicago.[1] Although Frazier was not talking explicitly about income when he used the phrase general culture, judging from his discussion, income seems to be a component of general culture. In spite of the meager evidence on the relation between income and family characteristics among black residential areas, the previous discussion of fertility and family patterns among black households provides a base for developing hypotheses about black residential areas.

Assume that black residential areas are differentiated according to the income of black households, that is, the residential areas are internally homogeneous according to income. Furthermore, assume that among black families, income is inversely related to fertility, positively related to presence of husband and wife, positively related to the formation of extended families, and inversely related to the formation of augmented families. Therefore I hypothesize that among black residential areas, median family income (FAMINC) is

[1]Frazier, The Negro Family in Chicago, p. 146.

1. Inversely related to per cent population under 18 (PCPP18).
2. Positively related to the per cent households which are husband-wife households (WIV/HD).
3. Positively related to ratio of other relatives of heads of households to heads of households (OTR/HD).
4. Inversely related to ratio of nonrelatives of heads of households to heads of households (NRL/HD).

In Table 43 are recorded the correlations of FAMINC with PCPP18, WIV/HD, OTR/HD, and NRL/HD for the sixteen cities.

TABLE 43

CORRELATION OF MEDIAN FAMILY INCOME (FAMINC) WITH PER CENT POPULATION UNDER 18 (PCPP18), PER CENT HOUSEHOLDS WHICH ARE HUSBAND-WIFE HOUSEHOLDS (WIV/HD), RATIO OF OTHER RELATIVES OF HEADS OF HOUSEHOLDS TO HEADS OF HOUSEHOLDS (OTR/HD), AND RATIO OF NONRELATIVES OF HEADS OF HOUSEHOLDS TO HEADS OF HOUSEHOLDS (NRL/HD)

City	PCPP18	WIV/HD	OTR/HD	NRL/HD
Atlanta	-.282[b]	.774[a]	.004	-.043
Baltimore	-.357[a]	.878[a]	.137	-.259[b]
Birmingham	-.082	.546[a]	.346[a]	-.260[b]
Cincinnati	-.490[a]	.821[a]	.640[a]	.568[a]
Columbia	-.059	.519[b]	-.274	-.144
Columbus	.133	.693[a]	-.165	-.494[b]
Detroit	-.145[b]	.721[a]	.112	-.289[a]
Kansas City	.504[a]	.921[a]	.594[a]	-.229
Los Angeles	-.004	.741[a]	-.054	-.158
Memphis	-.153	.490[a]	.148	-.008
Milwaukee	-.579[a]	.873[a]	.564[a]	.189
Philadelphia	-.202[b]	.846[a]	.228[a]	-.163[b]
Richmond	-.482[a]	.682[a]	.047	-.026
St. Louis	-.458[a]	.816[a]	.385[a]	-.168
Shreveport	-.369[b]	-.143	-.472[a]	.412[b]
Tampa-St. Petersburg	-.444[b]	.769[a]	.639[a]	.325

[a] Significant at 0.01 level.

[b] Significant at 0.05 level.

The highest correlations are between FAMINC and WIV/HD. These correlations are positive and significant at the 0.05 level in fifteen cities. Hence there is strong evidence for the hypothesis that FAMINC and WIV/HD are positively related among black residential areas. However, the correlations do not appear to be similar in all cities. In particular, the correlations for cities which are crudely classified as southern appear to be lower than non-southern cities. Therefore the Kruskal-Wallis rank test was used to examine whether or not the mean rank based on r of southern cities is smaller than would be expected if the ranks were selected at random without replacement.[1] The results of the analysis of the ranks of r's for FAMINC and WIV/HD are contained in Table 44. The null hypothesis that two groups (South and Non-South) come from the same population is rejected with probability less than 0.01. Thus the correlation between FAMINC and WIV/HD is lower in southern cities than in non-southern cities. However, I do not have a good explanation for this finding.

TABLE 44

RANK OF r BY REGION FOR FAMINC VS. WIV/HD

South		Non-South	
Rank	City	Rank	City
1	Shreveport	6	Columbus
2	Memphis	7	Detroit
3	Columbia	8	Los Angeles
4	Birmingham	11	St. Louis
5	Richmond	12	Cincinnati
9	Tampa-St. Petersburg	13	Philadelphia
10	Atlanta	14	Milwaukee
		15	Baltimore
		16	Kansas City

n = 7
R = 34

$\bar{R}$ = 4.857 uncorrected for continuity
$\sigma_{\bar{R}}^2$ = 3.6375

Unit normal deviate = -2.70.
One-tail test, $p < .01$.

Although few of the correlations of FAMINC with PCPP18, OTR/HD, and NRL/HD are very high, the correlations are in the direction hypothesized. First, ten of the eleven significant correlations between FAMINC and PCPP18 are negative. Thus there is some support for not rejecting the hypothesis that FAMINC is inversely related to PCPP18. Secondly, the signs of seven of the eight significant correlations between FAMINC and OTR/HD are positive as hypothesized and four of these seven correlations are greater than 0.500. However, the small number of significant correlations means that the evidence in support of the hypothesis must remain very tentative. Finally, the signs of twelve of the correlations between FAMINC and NRL/HD are negative as hypothesized.

[1]Kruskal and Wallis, "Use of Ranks in One-Criterion Variance Analysis," pp. 583-621.

However, only five of these are significant at the 0.05 level. In fact two significant correlations are positive. Thus at the level of the residential area, FAMINC and NRL/HD are not highly related. One explanation which can be offered is that, as mentioned in the previous chapter, only certain types of low income families may form augmented families. Therefore if low income families live in different residential areas according to family type, the correlation between FAMINC and NRL/HD will be low.

Since the relationship between FAMINC and the family type characteristics of WIV/HD, PCPP18, OTR/HD, and NRL/HD may be partly obscured by interrelations among the family type characteristics, the following regression model will be employed:

$$FAMINC = a + b(WIV/HD) + c(PCPP18) + d(OTR/HD) + e(NRL/HD) \qquad (26)$$

No causal assumptions are implied by using the family type characteristics as independent variables. The advantage to employing model 26 is that the relationship between one family type characteristic and FAMINC, while holding the other family type characteristics constant, can be examined.

In the results of the analysis of model 26 contained in Table 45 I recorded the simple correlation between FAMINC and WIV/HD on the first line for each city along with the r^2 assuming a simple linear relation between the two variables because WIV/HD revealed the highest correlations with FAMINC. In general the r^2 for model 26 is substantially larger than the r^2 relating FAMINC and WIV/HD. Judging from the partial correlation coefficients, it appears that PCPP18 adds an important independent contribution to the prediction of variation in FAMINC, while OTR/HD and NRL/HD do not add significantly to the prediction of FAMINC.

Turning to the individual partial correlations, when PCPP18, OTR/HD, and NRL/HD are held constant the partial correlation between FAMINC and WIV/HD is higher than the simple correlation in twelve of the sixteen cities. This result merely confirms the strong coincidence between FAMINC and WIV/HD among black residential areas. Perhaps of somewhat greater interest is the large increase in the negative partial correlation between FAMINC and PCPP18 compared with the simple correlation in Table 43 for the two variables. Holding OTR/HD and NRL/HD constant was probably the most important factor leading to the increase in correlation. The presence of large numbers of extended families which include young children as relatives in a residential area may tend to inflate PCPP18 while large numbers of augmented families with adults as nonrelatives may tend to lower PCPP18.[1] In Table 46 I have listed the correlations of PCPP18 with OTR/HD and NRL/HD. In some of the cities there is a moderately low correlation between PCPP18 and OTR/HD. More importantly, PCPP18 and NRL/HD have moderately high negative

---

[1]The reference point for per cent population under 18 (PCPP18) is that PCPP18 to be expected when only children of the husband and wife are included.

TABLE 45

SIMPLE CORRELATION OF MEDIAN FAMILY INCOME (FAMINC) WITH PER CENT HOUSEHOLDS WHICH ARE HUSBAND-WIFE HOUSEHOLDS (WIV/HD) AND PARTIAL CORRELATION OF FAMINC WITH WIV/HD, PER CENT POPULATION UNDER 18 (PCPP18), RATIO OF OTHER RELATIVES OF HEADS OF HOUSEHOLDS TO HEADS OF HOUSEHOLDS (OTR/HD), AND RATIO OF NONRELATIVES OF HEADS OF HOUSEHOLDS TO HEADS OF HOUSEHOLDS (NRL/HD)

City	Independent Variables[c]				r^2
	WIV/HD	PCPP18	OTR/HD	NRL/HD	
Atlanta	.774[a]				.599
	.907[a]	-.677[a]	-.363[b]	-.013	.850
Baltimore	.878[a]				.771
	.896[a]	-.673[a]	-.040	.002	.886
Birmingham	.546[a]				.298
	.708[a]	-.671[a]	.226	.034	.645
Cincinnati	.821[a]				.674
	.823[a]	-.775[a]	-.037	.108	.923
Columbia	.519[b]				.269
	.770[b]	.035	-.285	.451	.658
Columbus	.693[a]				.480
	.797[a]	-.735[a]	.023	-.085	.771
Detroit	.721[a]				.520
	.829[a]	-.733[a]	.074	-.192[b]	.784
Kansas City	.921[a]				.848
	.843[a]	-.253	.314	-.181	.869
Los Angeles	.741[a]				.549
	.877[a]	-.565[a]	-.261[b]	.172	.780
Memphis	.490[a]				.240
	.730[a]	-.462[a]	-.406[a]	.171	.580
Milwaukee	.873[a]				.762
	.833[a]	-.510	.355	.005	.888
Philadelphia	.846[a]				.716
	.895[a]	-.600[a]	-.088	.185	.853
Richmond	.682[a]				.465
	.859[a]	-.777[a]	-.019	.009	.863
St. Louis	.816[a]				.666
	.809[a]	-.717[a]	.222	-.119	.858
Shreveport	-.143				.020
	.566[a]	-.257	-.509[b]	.248	.487
Tampa-St. Petersburg	.769[a]				.591
	.745[a]	-.412	.160	.230	.790

[a]Significant at 0.01 level. [b]Significant at 0.05 level.

[c]Partial correlations on second line for each city.

TABLE 46

CORRELATION OF PER CENT POPULATION UNDER 18 (PCPP18) WITH RATIO OF OTHER RELATIVES OF HEADS OF HOUSEHOLDS TO HEADS OF HOUSEHOLDS (OTR/HD) AND RATIO OF NONRELATIVES OF HEADS OF HOUSEHOLDS TO HEADS OF HOUSEHOLDS (NRL/HD)

City	OTR/HD	NRL/HD
Atlanta	.235	-.469[a]
Baltimore	-.066	-.324[a]
Birmingham	.427[a]	-.669[a]
Cincinnati	.150	-.562[a]
Columbia	.802[a]	-.821[a]
Columbus	-.104	-.674[a]
Detroit	.198[b]	-.355[a]
Kansas City	.351[b]	-.277
Los Angeles	.036	-.687[a]
Memphis	.314[b]	-.743[a]
Milwaukee	-.222	-.697[a]
Philadelphia	.075	-.337[a]
Richmond	.078	-.574[a]
St. Louis	-.127	-.408[a]
Shreveport	.504[a]	-.785[a]
Tampa-St. Petersburg	-.158	-.714[a]

[a]Significant at 0.01 level.

[b]Significant at 0.05 level.

correlations. This provides some support for the contention that NRL/HD may understate PCPP18. Whatever the underlying factors, FAMINC and PCPP18 are inversely related among black residential areas. That is, the higher the median family income in a black residential area the lower the proportion of the population under 18 years old.

Finally, the low partial correlations of FAMINC with OTR/HD and NRL/HD are further indications that FAMINC and these two aspects of family type characteristics reveal few significant associations among black residential areas when other variables are held constant.

CHAPTER VII

CONCLUSIONS: TOWARDS A SOCIAL GEOGRAPHY OF BLACK RESIDENTIAL AREAS

The overriding hypothesis of this study was that the spatial variation in the characteristics of housing among black residential areas is a significant element in the spatial variation in the characteristics of black households in cities. The hypothesis was approached by reviewing and developing ideas on individual household residential choice. From these ideas of residential choice hypotheses concerning the spatial variation in the characteristics of black households in cities were deduced. In general, the overriding hypothesis of the study was substantiated. The spatial variation of black households according to characteristics such as income and family type is highly associated with the spatial variation in the characteristics of housing available to black homeseekers in black residential areas. This occurs in spite of the obvious constraints by whites on black residential choices. The major results can be summarized in a series of simple graphic models which portray the relationship between the variation in the characteristics of housing and the variation in the characteristics of black households. In the models the assumption is that housing characteristics within each of the black residential areas as defined (census tracts) are relatively homogeneous. Therefore the variation in the characteristics of black housing is that variation occurring among black residential areas. Furthermore, the assumption is that the black household, in making its residential decision, is confronted with a given stock of housing. I am not concerned with the characteristics of black households moving into "white" residential areas.

Models of Black Residential Areas

Assume that the price of housing paid by a black household is a positive function of its income. Therefore in graphic model 27 the median family income of a black residential area is a positive function of the median value of owner occupied units and also of the median rent of renter occupied units (Figure 8).[1] Thus the higher the price of housing in

---

[1]Graphic model 27 is a graphical combination of statistical models 8 and 9 in Chapter IV.

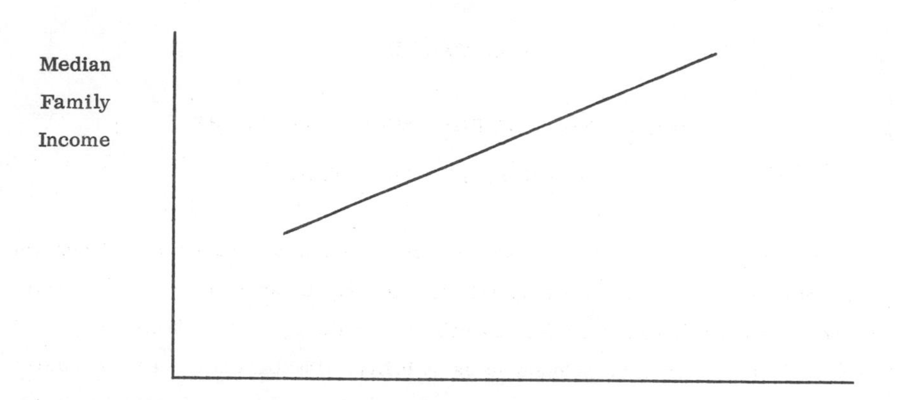

Fig. 8.--Model 27: Relation Between Income and Price of Housing among Black Residential Areas in Cities

a residential area the higher the income of the black households who choose to live there. There are two qualifications to model 27. First, the model is weakest in describing the relationship between median family income and median value of owner occupied units in southern cities. Secondly, the relationship between median family income and median value of owner occupied units tends to be weaker than the relationship between median family income and median rent of renter occupied units. Nevertheless the significant fact is that income and price of housing are positively related among black residential areas.

In model 28 assume that the decision to own is positively related to income. Therefore the percentage of the occupied units which are owned in a black residential area is positively related to median family income of the black households (Figure 9). Generally model 28 is somewhat more applicable to non-southern cities than it is to southern cities. Nevertheless, Frazier's contention that homeownership is an important differentiating characteristic of black residential areas is supported by the findings in this study.[1]

Assuming that the quality of housing purchased by a black household is positively related to its income, then in graphic model 29 the median family income of a black residential area is a positive function of the quality of housing in the residential area. The

---

[1] Frazier, The Negro Family in Chicago, pp. 126-46.

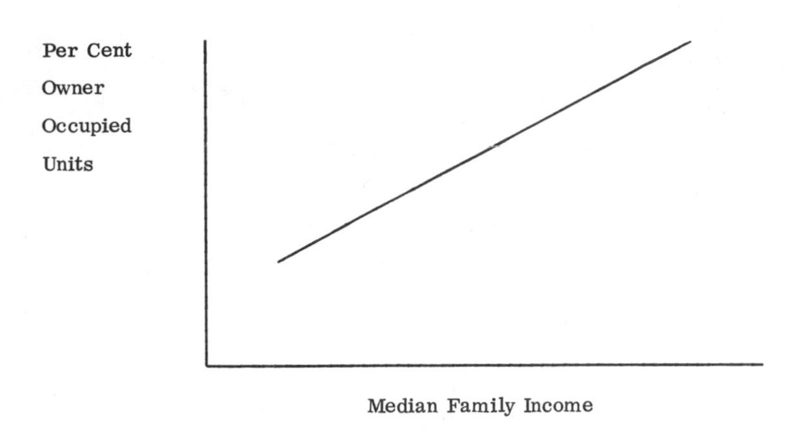

Fig. 9.--Model 28: Relation Between Per Cent Owner Occupied Units and Median Family Income among Black Residential Areas

relation between income and quality of housing among black residential areas depicted in Figure 10 does not support the often casual description of black residential areas as being undifferentiated "slums." On the contrary, model 29 asserts that given spatial variation in the quality of housing, the higher the quality of housing the higher the income of the black households who choose to live there. The relationship between income and quality of housing holds equally as strongly in southern cities as in non-southern cities. This results in spite of the fact that the housing occupied by Afro-Americans in southern cities is significantly poorer in quality than housing occupied by Afro-Americans in non-southern cities.

As is evident, value and rent of housing, rates of owner occupancy, and quality of housing are all positively related to income. Each characteristic of housing is a significant element in the differentiation of black residential areas, though they are not, of course, independent of each other.

Regularities also exist in the relationships between the spatial distribution of family characteristics and the spatial distribution of housing characteristics. Preference for living in single family dwellings seems to vary with the stage in the life cycle of the family. Families with children are especially likely to want to live in single family dwellings. However, since single family dwellings are generally larger and more expensive than

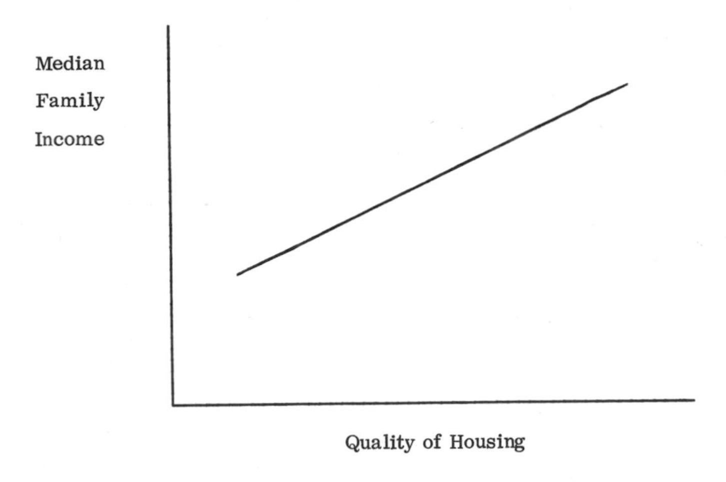

Fig. 10.--Model 29: Relation Between Median Family Income and Quality of Housing among Black Residential Areas

apartments, the capability of living in a single family dwelling is partly dependent upon income. Therefore, in model 30 the per cent of the population under 18 years old in a black residential area is a positive function of the per cent single family dwellings, holding median family income constant (Figure 11).

A related graphic model (model 31) which summarizes the relationship between life cycle and housing is contained in Figure 12. In this model assume that the larger the number of children under 18 years in a black family the more likely the family will want to own its dwelling. However, ownership is partly related to family income. Therefore in model 31 the per cent of the population under 18 years in a black residential area is positively related to the per cent owner occupied dwellings, holding median family income constant. This model is more applicable to southern cities than to non-southern cities.

Among black households with both husband and wife present there may be a strong demand for owner occupancy. Based on the present findings, it is suggested for model 32 that the per cent black households with both husband and wife present in a black residential area is positively related to the per cent owner occupied units (Figure 13). This relationship continues to hold true even when the effects of median family income on per cent owner occupied dwellings are removed.

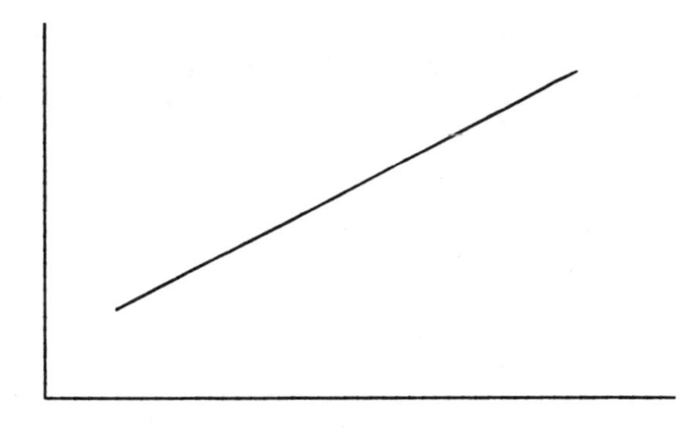

Fig. 11.--Model 30: Relation Between Per Cent Population under 18 Years and Per Cent Single Family Dwellings Holding Median Family Income Constant among Black Residential Areas

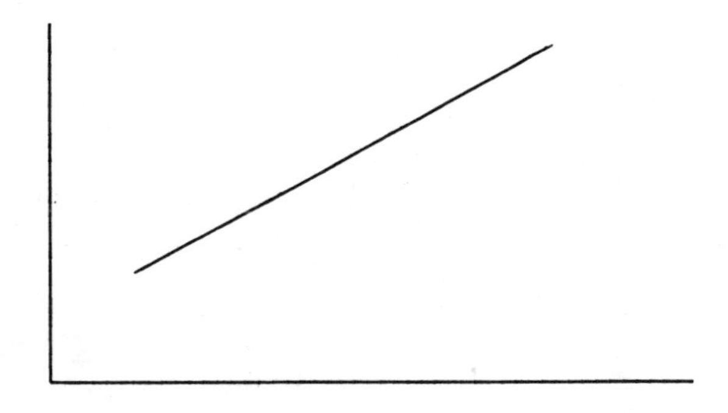

Fig. 12.--Model 31: Relation Between Per Cent Population under 18 Years and Per Cent Owner Occupied Dwellings Holding Median Family Income Constant among Black Residential Areas

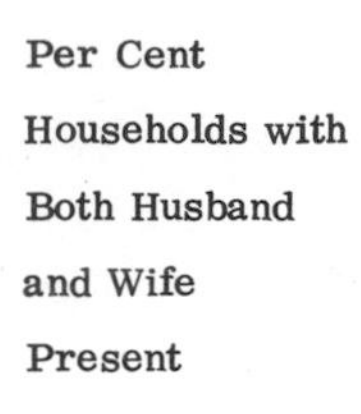

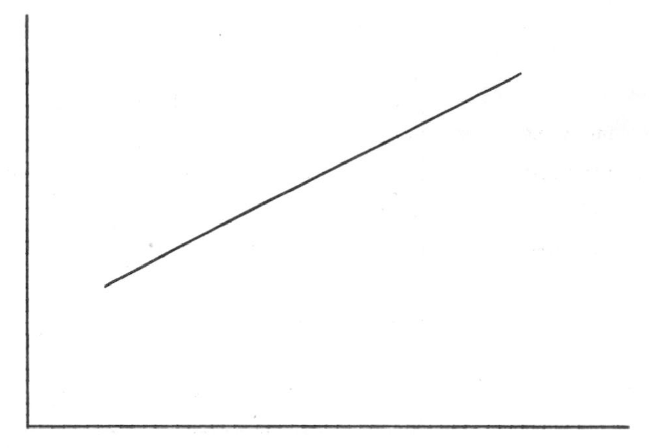

Fig. 13.--Model 32: Relation Between Per Cent Households with Both Husband and Wife Present and Per Cent Owner Occupied Dwellings among Black Residential Areas

Spatial Variations in Housing Stock

In these graphic models no mention is made of the spatial distribution of housing characteristics within cities except to assert that housing characteristics are relatively homogeneous within residential areas. Yet, as discussed at various points in this study, regularities exist in the spatial distribution of housing characteristics within cities. Therefore the basic ideas concerning these spatial regularities will now be briefly reviewed.

Implicit in Burgess' formulation of the growth of the city is the notion that high income households move to the periphery of cities where they can obtain new housing which meets their needs while the low income households settle in the more deteriorated, relatively low cost, housing near the center of the city.[1] Hawley, somewhat more explicitly, postulated essentially the same spatial pattern of housing. He argued that new housing, which is generally better equipped for families than old housing, is built on the periphery. Because of its more desirable qualities, this new housing commands higher rents than old housing. Hence Hawley claimed that the rental values for housing increase

---

[1]Burgess, "The Growth of the City: An Introduction to a Research Project," pp. 47-62.

with distance from the city center.[1] In the more rigorous formulations of Alonso and Muth, the conclusions are essentially the same. Namely, high income families tend to live on the periphery of cities and low income families near the center of cities.[2]

Other studies claim that the rental value of housing is distributed sectorally.[3] This need not be inconsistent with the above formulation if within each sector (high, middle, and low rent) there are gradients such that rental value increases with distance from the CBD.

Given the fact that consumption of housing increases with income and that new housing is built on the periphery of cities, then the spatial pattern of housing is as follows:

1. Quality, size, value, and rent of housing increase with distance from the city center (CBD).
2. Age of housing decreases with distance from the CBD.

Furthermore, Alonso argues that the higher the income the higher the consumption of land.[4] Since the high income households move to the periphery we would expect that population density declines with distance from the CBD. In fact Muth has demonstrated empirically this decline in density with increasing distance from the CBD.[5] Therefore one could infer that

3. The proportion of single family dwellings in residential areas increases with distance from the CBD.[6]

To the extent that quality, size, value, and rent of housing increase with distance from the CBD and age of housing declines with distance from the CBD, then for graphic model 33 it is proposed that the median family income of black households increases with distance from the CBD (Figure 14). Based on findings in this study model 33 seems to apply principally to non-southern cities. Furthermore the proportion of households with both husband and wife present in black residential areas increases with distance from the CBD so that model 33 also describes this relationship.

---

[1]Amos H. Hawley, Human Ecology (New York: Ronald Press Company, 1950), p. 281.

[2]Alonso, Location and Land Use, pp. 76-100; and Muth, Cities and Housing, pp. 18-31.

[3]For example, see Homer Hoyt, The Structure and Growth of Residential Neighborhoods in American Cities (Washington: U. S. Government Printing Office, 1939).

[4]Alonso, Location and Land Use, p. 109.

[5]Muth, Cities and Housing, pp. 141-45.

[6]This pattern corresponds to Burgess' description of the variation in housing type in the concentric zones about the city. See Burgess, "The Growth of the City: An Introduction to a Research Project."

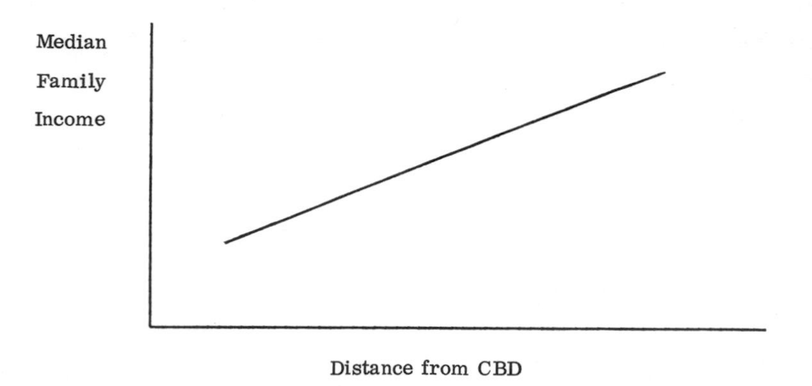

Fig. 14.--Model 33: Relation Between Median Family Income and Distance from the CBD among Black Residential Areas in Non-Southern Cities

However, in southern cities the median family income of black households increases with distance from the CBD, and then income declines after some distance i from the CBD. This spatial pattern is termed model 34 (Figure 15). In southern cities those black residential areas beyond some distance i from the CBD are probably poor rural black settlements on the periphery of southern cities. These settlements are seldom found around non-southern cities.

The spatial dispersion of black residential areas also seems to be a factor in the spatial variation of the per cent of the population under 18 years with respect to the CBD. To the extent that the proportion of single family dwellings in residential areas increases with distance from the CBD, then in model 35 it is suggested that the per cent of the population under 18 years should increase with distance from the CBD in black residential areas (Figure 16). However, my empirical analyses demonstrated that model 35 is only applicable to southern cities.

An alternative model for non-southern cities which will be termed model 36 is illustrated in Figure 17. In this model the high per cent of the population under 18 years close to the CBD may identify public housing for low income families with children. Yet model 36 has limited applicability in non-southern cities. The model fit only three of the nine non-southern cities in this study, Baltimore, Kansas City, and St. Louis. Perhaps

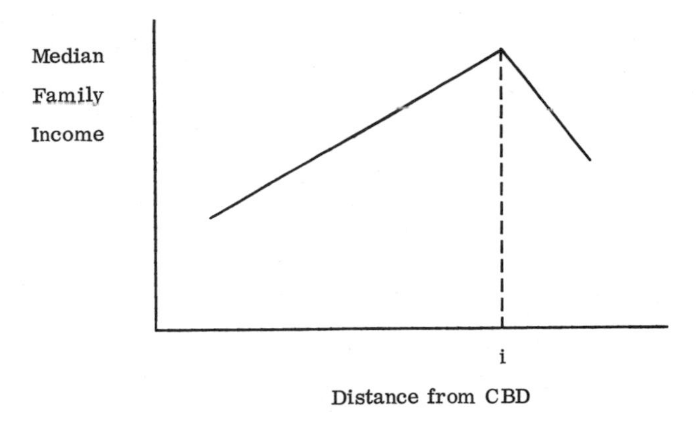

Fig. 15.--Model 34: Relation Between Median Family Income and Distance from the CBD among Black Residential Areas in Southern Cities

the reason neither the simple linear model nor the curvilinear model adequately describes the variation in per cent black population under 18 years with respect to the CBD in most non-southern cities is that Afro-Americans in these cities have been restricted to residential areas relatively close to the CBD. Hence black families with children do not have access to a wide range of housing in low density areas of the city.

The explanation for the different spatial patterns in southern and non-southern cities was discussed in previous chapters. To summarize, in many southern cities black residential areas are dispersed throughout the city. In part this pattern is a remnant of the times when slaves lived in the backyards of the slaveowners. Of course black households are still highly segregated from white households in southern cities. Furthermore, rural black settlements surrounding southern cities are incorporated into the city as the city expands. The dispersed nature of these settlements provides a base for the dispersed pattern of black residential areas. However, in non-southern cities Afro-Americans have seldom lived in rural settlements on the periphery of cities. Instead the first black inhabitants migrated from the South and settled near the CBD. White constraints on black households retarded the movement of these black families to the periphery. Therefore a wide range of housing in low density areas is not available to black

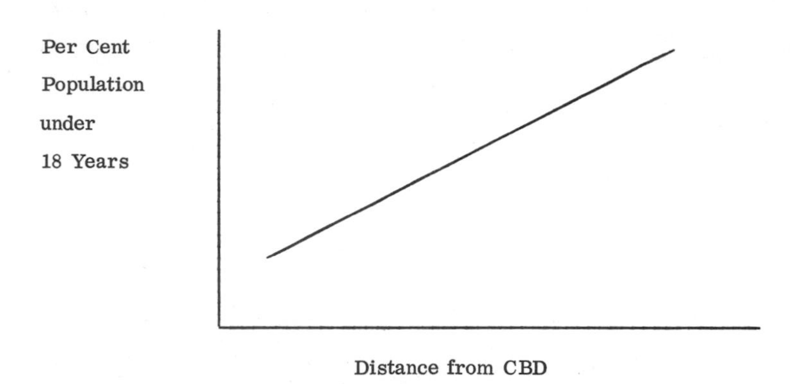

Fig. 16.--Model 35: Relation Between Per Cent Population under 18 Years and Distance from CBD among Black Residential Areas in Southern Cities

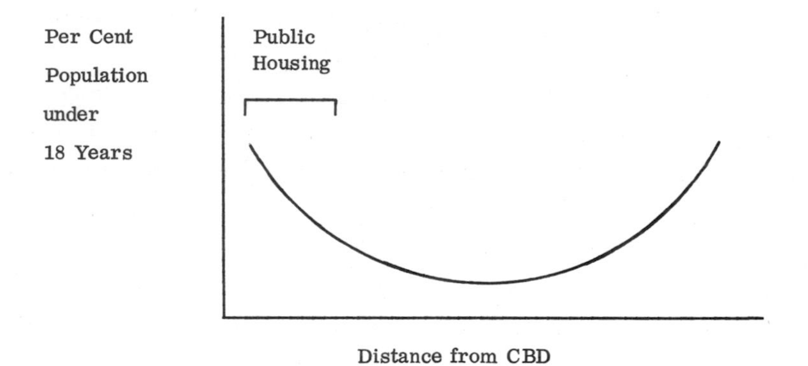

Fig. 17.--Model 36: Relation Between Per Cent Population under 18 Years and Distance from CBD among Black Residential Areas in Some Non-Southern Cities

households in non-southern cities, and particularly, low-income dependent populations are concentrated in central-city public housing rather than diffused in peripheral rural housing.

The results which have been summarized apply only to black residential areas. Further insight into the differentiation of black residential areas can be gained by comparing these results for black residential areas with studies of white residential areas. I now turn to this comparison.

Comparison Between Ecology of Black Residential Areas and Ecology of White Residential Areas

On the basis of the review of the literature so far available on residential choice,[1] one could conclude that there is a rough correspondence between the residential choices of black households and the residential choices of white households when families of similar socioeconomic status and family type characteristics are compared. The significant exception, however, is that black households are frequently restrained from fulfilling their residential choices by white constraints. Therefore, an important question is to what extent white constraints on black housing choice change the ecology of black residential areas from that ecology which would be expected in the absence of racial constraints. Some bases of comparison which can be used are the social area analyses and factorial ecologies of American cities which are, for the most part, studies of white residential areas. In effect, these studies describe the differentiation of residential areas in the absence of racial constraints on housing choices.

White residential areas

As discussed in the previous chapter, reviewers of the literature on social area analysis and factorial ecology have concluded that there are at least two fundamental and relatively independent dimensions to the differentiation of residential areas within cities of "western" culture and American cities in particular. These dimensions include socio-economic status and family status, with ethnic status or segregation occurring as a third separate dimension in some cities.[2] Exceptions to this general pattern of American cities have primarily been noted in southern cities.[3]

---

[1]The emphasis on "so far available" is important because, as my review of black residential choice reveals, our understanding of black residential choice is very superficial.

[2]Abu-Lughod, "Testing the Theory of Social Area Analysis: The Ecology of Cairo, Egypt," pp. 198-212; and Murdie, Factorial Ecology of Metropolitan Toronto, 1951-1961, pp. 17-31.

[3]Van Arsdol, Camilleri, and Schmid, "The Generality of Urban Social Area Indexes," pp. 277-84.

The socioeconomic status dimension is generally characterized by such variables as occupation, education, income, rent, and quality of housing. Thus a residential area characterized as high socioeconomic status would contain residents with high occupational status, advanced levels of education, high income, high rent, and good quality housing. The family status dimension is characterized by variables such as fertility, women in the labor force, and single family dwellings. A residential area classified as high family status (early stage in life cycle) would contain women with high fertility and low rates of participation in the labor force as well as a high percentage of single family dwellings. Finally, the ethnic status or segregation dimension is usually indexed by the variable, per cent of population Afro-American. However, the segregation dimension may have variables indexing socioeconomic status or family status associated with it.[1] The crucial point in terms of this discussion is the assertion that the socioeconomic status and family status dimensions are relatively independent of each other. Given such an assertion for white residential areas, what is the situation among black residential areas?

Black residential areas

The results reported in this study indicate that median family income (FAMINC) is positively related to median value of owner occupied units (VALOWN), median rent of renter occupied units (MDRENT), per cent owner occupied units (PCONOC), and per cent sound units (PCSOND). Since the above variables are indicators of socioeconomic status, a socioeconomic status dimension seems to exist among black residential areas. At the same time, it was found that the per cent of the population under 18 (PCPP18) was positively related to per cent single family dwellings (PCSFDW) when FAMINC was held constant. Thus there is some evidence for a family status dimension among black residential areas as defined by the social area analysts and factorial ecologists. However, it was also reported that FAMINC was positively related to per cent households which are husband-wife households (WIV/HD) and inversely related to PCPP18. If WIV/HD and PCPP18 are assumed to be indicators of family status and FAMINC is assumed to be a surrogate for socioeconomic status, then there is some evidence for suggesting that family status and socioeconomic status are related among black residential areas. This is

---

[1]Wendell Bell, "Economic, Family, and Ethnic Status: An Empirical Test," American Sociological Review, XX (February, 1955), 45-52; Philip H. Rees, "The Factorial Ecology of Metropolitan Chicago, 1960" (unpublished Master's dissertation, Department of Geography, University of Chicago, 1968); Calvin F. Schmid and Kiyoshi Tagashira, "Ecological and Demographic Indices: A Methodological Analysis," Demography, I (1964), 194-211; Frank L. Sweetser, "Factor Structure as Ecological Structure in Helsinki and Boston," Acta Sociologica, VIII (1965), 205-25; and Van Arsdol, Camilleri, and Schmid, "The Generality of Urban Social Area Indexes."

different from the situation among white residential areas where family status and socioeconomic status are said to be relatively independent. It is doubtful whether racial differences in the relationship between family status and socioeconomic status at the level of the residential area can be explained by racial differences in this relationship at the household level; in the previous chapter fertility, an indicator of family status, was reported as being inversely related to socioeconomic status among both whites and blacks. If this is the case, and if residential choices of blacks and whites are similar, then to what extent are white constraints on black housing choice responsible for the association between family status and socioeconomic status among black residential areas?

Bases for association between socioeconomic status and family status among black residential areas

White constraints

A set of propositions developed by Abu-Lughod relating to the circumstances under which socioeconomic status (social rank) and family status variables are related or are not related among residential areas provide a framework for examining the effects of white constraints on the association between socioeconomic status and family status among black residential areas. She states:

> Granted a situation in which both family and social rank variables are reflected in the ecological pattern, under what circumstances would one expect these variables to lie on the same vector or to lie upon somewhat separate vectors? A necessary but not sufficient condition of the former is that social rank and family type be correlated, that the "typical" family of one social class be significantly different from the "typical" family of another class. Conversely, a necessary but not sufficient condition of the latter is that there be no major overpowering linkages between class on the one hand, and such familism variables as fertility, completed family size, and tendency to remain within extended households on the other hand. These conditions exist within the realm of social space. They are necessary but not sufficient because they fail to take into account the character of physical space. Thus, even given some relationship between class and family type, it would still be possible to have "familism" variables somewhat disassociated from socioeconomic rank variables if two further conditions were present: (1) if stages in the family cycle were clearly distinguished from one another, each stage being associated with a change in residence; and (2) if sufficiently large subareas within the city offered, at all economic levels, highly specialized housing accommodations suited to families at particular points in their natural cycle of growth and decline. A third condition is also assumed, namely, cultural values permitting and favoring mobility to maximize housing efficiency, unencumbered by the "unnatural" frictions of sentiment, local attachments, or restrictive regulations.[1]

Following Abu-Lughod's discussion, I suggest that the most important effect of white housing constraints is to limit the range of specialized housing accommodations

---

[1]Abu-Lughod, "Testing the Theory of Social Area Analysis: The Ecology of Cairo, Egypt," pp. 208-9.

suitable for black households at various stages in their life cycle. Given their incomes, those households least likely to obtain housing appropriate to their stage in life cycle are probably the middle and upper income households. Whereas the low income black household may not find suitable housing strictly because of its income, regardless of their income the middle and upper income households are kept from expressing their housing choices by a system of white constraints. For example, suppose there are two sets of middle income black households: middle-age households without children and young households with children. Given basic principles of residential choice discussed earlier, one would expect that the middle-age households without children might prefer apartment dwellings close to the center of the city while the young households with children would prefer single family dwellings near the periphery of the city. However, because of white resistance, the young families with children cannot obtain single family dwellings near the periphery of the city. Therefore both the middle-age couples and the young families must live together in multi-family dwellings near the center of the city. Hence within some or all income brackets, black residential areas may not be highly differentiated by age of family. Therefore the relation between fertility and socioeconomic status existing at the level of the individual black household also appears at the level of the black residential area.

Extended families

Another factor affecting the association between socioeconomic status and family status among black residential areas may be the prevalence of extended families among black households. In urbanized areas the ratio of other relatives of head to heads of households is 0.51 among nonwhites (mainly Afro-Americans) and only 0.19 among whites.[1] Assuming that the above ratios are crude indicators of the incidence of extended families, then the extended family is significantly more important among black households than among white households. The prevalence of the extended family among black households means that the stages of the family life cycle are not clearly distinguished from each other within many black households. Instead, different stages in the life cycle of the family are all present at the same time in the household. Hence the demand for housing accommodations does not vary according to stages in the life of the family but instead remains relatively constant. In such a situation Abu-Lughod implies that family status and socioeconomic status may not exist as independent dimensions.[2] Instead, given a preference

---

[1] U. S., Bureau of the Census, U. S. Census of Population: 1960, Subject Reports, Persons by Family Characteristics, Table 4a, p. 33.

[2] Abu-Lughod, "Testing the Theory of Social Area Analysis: The Ecology of Cairo, Egypt," pp. 208-9.

by black households for living near other households of comparable income, the result is an association between family status and socioeconomic status among black residential areas.

Validity of using social area analyses and factorial ecologies as bases of comparison

Although I have made use of social area analyses and factorial ecologies of American cities as bases for comparing the ecology of black residential areas, this action can be seriously questioned from at least two standpoints. First, although Afro-Americans comprise a relatively small proportion of the total population of many American cities, their presence still has an effect on the results of the social area analyses and factorial ecologies. Therefore these studies may not truly reflect the ecology of white residential areas.

Secondly, and perhaps more importantly, the social area analyses and factorial ecologies have different statistical bases than the techniques employed in this study. These differences may have a significant impact on the validity of making comparisons between studies employing the different statistical techniques. I employed regression and correlation analysis while studies of social area analysis and factorial ecology usually employed some form of factor analysis model. The following remarks concerning social area analyses and factorial ecologies apply only to those studies employing some form of factor analysis model.[1]

The common practice in studies using factor analysis is to report in matrix form the correlations of the variables with the factors. This matrix is used to interpret the data and seldom is reference made to the original correlation matrix of the variables. The factor is usually interpreted by referring to the variables which have their highest correlations with that factor. However, the correlations between the variables and the factors are not the same as the correlations between the original variables. Factors are hypothetical constructs which are usually defined in terms of several variables, and it is these hypothetical constructs with which the variables are correlated.[2]

Therefore, when mention is made that there are at least two relatively independent dimensions to the differentiation of American cities, socioeconomic status and family status, this refers to the hypothetical constructs. This claim does not refer to the relations between the individual variables indexing the two constructs. Even when the constructs

---

[1]All of the social area analyses and factorial ecologies which have been referred to in this chapter employed some form of factor analysis model.

[2]Harry H. Harman, Modern Factor Analysis (2d ed., rev.; Chicago: University of Chicago Press, 1967), pp. 14-21.

are said to be independent (uncorrelated), variables highly correlated with different constructs are not necessarily uncorrelated. For example, income and fertility are highly correlated with separate dimensions in studies of white residential areas. However, this does not mean that the variables are necessarily uncorrelated with each other. Thus it is possible that the variables, income and fertility, may be similarly related among black and white residential areas.

Hence my comparison of the ecology of black residential areas, derived from a regression and correlation analysis, with the ecology of white residential areas, derived from a factor analysis model, must be interpreted with caution. A more satisfactory solution to the problem would be to employ the same statistical technique on studies of black and white residential areas. As yet, however, these comparable studies do not exist.

Limitations of Study and Suggestions for Further Research

In this study I assumed that the black household in making its residential decision is confronted with a given stock of housing. In general it was suggested that the characteristics of black households who choose to live in a residential area are a function of the characteristics of the housing in the residential area. This follows from the residential choice process of the black household. However, white constraints on black residential choice limit the range of housing characteristics available to black households. Therefore the relationships between household and housing characteristics among black residential areas which were identified may not represent the relationships that would exist in the absence of constraints.

Another limitation of this study is that there was no control for the fact that households can influence the characteristics of the housing stock in a residential area, especially value, rent, and quality. For example, assume a set of households moves into a residential area because the price of housing is appropriate to their budgets. Now if a family wants to sell its dwelling, the price the family can obtain is partly affected by the characteristics of the other households in the residential area. This results because part of the value of housing depends upon the favorable or unfavorable characteristics of the surrounding residents. To isolate the influences of households on housing characteristics in residential areas would require a careful analysis of changes in household and housing characteristics over time.

This study tended to operate at a very general level of inquiry because so little is known about the relationships between household and housing characteristics among black residential areas. Hopefully it provides a basis for in-depth studies. Perhaps the following lines of research may increase our understanding of the spatial variation of black households among black residential areas within cities.

1. Studies of individual black residential choice, involving a sample survey approach, are needed.
2. Components of socioeconomic status which are most relevant for the differentiation of black residential areas need to be identified. Income may not be the most important factor.
3. The mechanism of the changeover from white occupancy to black occupancy needs further analysis, since at least within non-southern cities this is the major means by which the black housing supply is expanded and a greater variety of housing types and residential areas become available.
4. Finally, we need to understand the dynamic character of black residential areas. This involves research on the changing population and changing housing characteristics of black residential areas.

In spite of the massive body of literature, we know relatively little concerning the role of Afro-Americans as an integral part of an evolving urban system. As was evident in the dates of specific references to literature on Afro-Americans in cities in this study, most of the important studies are over twenty years old. Too much research on Afro-Americans has been devoted to their contact with the white population to the neglect of basic research on Afro-Americans as a distinctive part of American society.

BIBLIOGRAPHY

Residential Choice and Intra-Urban Mobility

Brown, Lawrence A., and Moore, Eric G. "The Intra-Urban Migration Process: A Perspective." Geografiska Annaler, forthcoming.

Galt, John E. "The Residential Distribution of the Employees of Argonne National Laboratory: Patterns and Implications." Unpublished Master's dissertation, Department of Geography, University of Chicago, 1968.

Heiges, Harvey E. "Nere-Migration in Seattle, 1962-1967." Unpublished Ph.D. dissertation, Department of Geography, University of Washington, 1968.

Lansing, John B., and Mueller, Eva. Residential Location and Urban Mobility. [Ann Arbor]: Survey Research Center, Institute for Social Research, The University of Michigan, 1964.

Moore, Eric G. "The Structure of Intra-Urban Movement Rates: An Ecological Model." Urban Studies, VI (February, 1969), 17-33.

Peterson, George L. "A Model of Preference: Quantitative Analysis of the Perception of the Visual Appearance of Residential Neighborhoods." Journal of Regional Science, VII (Summer, 1967), 19-31.

Rossi, Peter H. Why Families Move. Glencoe, Ill.: The Free Press, 1955.

Simmons, James W. "Changing Residence in the City: A Review of Intraurban Mobility." Geographical Review, LVIII (October, 1968), 622-51.

Wolpert, Julian. "Behavioral Aspects of the Decision to Migrate." Papers of the Regional Science Association, XV (1965), 159-69.

Studies of Afro-Americans

Billingsley, Andrew. Black Families in White America. Englewood Cliffs, N.J.: Prentice-Hall, Inc., 1968.

Drake, St. Clair, and Cayton, Horace R. Black Metropolis. Vol. II. Rev. ed. New York: Harper & Row, 1962.

DuBois, W. E. B. The Philadelphia Negro. Publications of the University of Pennsylvania: Political Economy and Public Law, No. 14. Philadelphia: University of Pennsylvania, 1899. Reprinted, New York: Schocken Books, 1967.

Duncan, Otis D., and Duncan, Beverly. The Negro Population of Chicago. Chicago: The University of Chicago Press, 1957.

Frazier, E. Franklin. The Negro Family in Chicago. Chicago: The University of Chicago Press, 1932.

________. The Negro in the United States. New York: The Macmillan Company, 1949.

Kiser, Clyde V. "Fertility Trends and Differentials among Non-Whites in the United States." Milbank Memorial Fund Quarterly, XXXVI (April, 1958), 149-97.

Osofsky, Gilbert. Harlem: The Making of a Ghetto. New York: Harper & Row, 1966. Harper Torchbook ed.; New York: Harper & Row, 1968.

Schnore, Leo F. "Social Class Segregation among Nonwhites in Metropolitan Centers." Demography, II (1965), 126-33.

Spear, Allan H. Black Chicago: The Making of a Negro Ghetto, 1890-1920. Chicago: The University of Chicago Press, 1967.

Taeuber, Karl E., and Taeuber, Alma F. Negroes in Cities. Chicago: Aldine Publishing Co., 1965.

Wade, Richard C. Slavery in the Cities: The South 1820-1860. London: Oxford University Press, 1964.

Woofter, T. J., Jr., ed. Negro Problems in Cities. Garden City, N.Y.: Doubleday, Doran & Co., Inc., 1928.

Housing and Race

Berry, Brian J. L., et al. "Down from the Summit." Unpublished paper, Center for Urban Studies, University of Chicago, 1969.

Caplan, Eleanor K., and Wolf, Eleanor P. "Factors Affecting Racial Change in Two Middle Income Housing Areas." Phylon, XXI (1960), 225-33.

Duncan, Beverly, and Hauser, Philip M. Housing a Metropolis--Chicago. Glencoe, Ill.: The Free Press of Glencoe, 1960.

Editors of the Journal of Housing. "Six Goals for a Program of Low-Income Housing." The Journal of Housing, XX (May, 1963), 259-65. Reprinted in Wheaton, William L. C.; Milgram, Grace; and Meyerson, Margy E.; eds. Urban Housing. New York: The Free Press, 1966. Pp. 241-45.

Glazer, Nathan, and McEntire, Davis, eds. Studies in Housing and Minority Groups. Berkeley and Los Angeles: University of California Press, 1960.

Grier, Eunice, and Grier, George. "Market Characteristics in Interracial Housing." Journal of Social Issues, XIII, No. 4 (1957), 50-59.

Gries, John M., and Ford, James, eds. Negro Housing. Report of the Committee on Negro Housing, The President's Conference on Home Building and Home Ownership. Washington, D.C.: National Capital Press, Inc., 1932.

Maisel, Sherman J., and Winnick, Louis. "Family Housing Expenditures: Elusive Laws and Intrusive Variances." Proceedings of the Conference on Consumption and Saving. Edited by Irwin Friend and Robert Jones. 2 vols. [Philadelphia]: University of Pennsylvania, 1960. I. Pp. 359-435.

Meyerson, Martin; Terrett, Barbara; and Wheaton, William L. C. Housing, People, and Cities. New York: McGraw-Hill Book Company, 1962.

Ohio Civil Rights Commission. Discrimination in Housing in Ohio. Columbus, Ohio, 1963.

Rapkin, Chester. "Price Discrimination Against Negroes in the Rental Housing Market." Essays in Urban Land Economics. Real Estate Research Program. Los Angeles: University of California, 1966. Pp. 333-45.

Reid, Margaret G. Housing and Income. Chicago: The University of Chicago Press, 1962.

Schietinger, E. F. "Racial Succession and Value of Small Residential Properties." American Sociological Review, XVI (December, 1951), 832-35.

Stetler, Henry G. Racial Integration in Private Residential Neighborhoods in Connecticut. Hartford, Conn.: Commission on Civil Rights, 1957.

Taeuber, Karl E. "The Effect of Income Redistribution on Racial Residential Segregation." Urban Affairs Quarterly, IV (September, 1968), 5-14.

Tilly, Charles; Jackson, Wagner D.; and Kay, Barry. Race and Residence in Wilmington, Delaware. New York : Bureau of Publications, Teachers College, Columbia University, 1965.

Watts, Lewis G., et al. The Middle-Income Negro Family Faces Urban Renewal. Waltham, Mass.: Brandeis University, 1964.

Weaver, Robert C. The Negro Ghetto. New York: Harcourt, Brace and Company, 1948.

Wolf, Eleanor P. "The Invasion-Succession Sequence as a Self-Fulfilling Prophecy." Journal of Social Issues, XIII, No. 4 (1957), 7-20.

Urban Structure

Abu-Lughod, Janet L. "Testing the Theory of Social Area Analysis: The Ecology of Cairo, Egypt." American Sociological Review, XXXIV (April, 1969), 198-212.

Alonso, William. Location and Land Use. Cambridge: Harvard University Press, 1964.

Bell, Wendell. "Economic, Family and Ethnic Status: An Empirical Test." American Sociological Review, XX (February, 1955), 45-52.

Berry, Brian J. L. Commercial Structure and Commercial Blight. Department of Geography Research Paper No. 85. Chicago: Department of Geography, University of Chicago, 1963.

Berry, Brian J. L., and Rees, Philip H. "The Factorial Ecology of Calcutta." American Journal of Sociology, LXXIV (March, 1969), 445-91.

Burgess, Ernest W. "The Growth of the City: An Introduction to a Research Project." The City. Edited by Robert E. Park, Ernest W. Burgess, and R. D. McKenzie. Chicago: University of Chicago Press, 1925.

Burns, Leland S., and Harman, Alvin J. The Complex Metropolis. Part 6; Profile of the Los Angeles Metropolis, Its People and Its Homes; Research Report No. 9; Housing, Real Estate, and Urban Land Studies Program. Los Angeles: University of California, 1968.

Hoyt, Homer. The Structure and Growth of Residential Neighborhoods in American Cities. Washington: U. S. Government Printing Office, 1939.

Meyer, David R. "Classification of SMSA's Based upon Characteristics of Their Nonwhite Populations." Classification of Cities: New Methods and Evolving Uses. Edited by Brian J. L. Berry. International City Managers Association and Resources for the Future, forthcoming.

Meyer, J. R.; Kain, J. F.; and Wohl, M. The Urban Transportation Problem. Cambridge: Harvard University Press, 1965.

Murdie, Robert A. Factorial Ecology of Metropolitan Toronto, 1951-1961. Department of Geography Research Paper No. 116. Chicago: Department of Geography, University of Chicago, 1969.

Muth, Richard F. Cities and Housing. Chicago: The University of Chicago Press, 1969.

Rees, Philip H. "The Factorial Ecology of Metropolitan Chicago, 1960." Unpublished Master's dissertation, Department of Geography, University of Chicago, 1968.

Schmid, Calvin F., and Tagashira, Kiyoshi. 'Ecological and Demographic Indices: A Methodological Analysis." Demography, I (1964), 194-211.

Sweetser, Frank L. "Factor Structure as Ecological Structure in Helsinki and Boston." Acta Sociologica, VIII (1965), 205-25.

Van Arsdol, Maurice D., Jr.; Camilleri, Santo F.; and Schmid, Calvin F. "The Generality of Urban Social Area Indexes." American Sociological Review, XXIII (June, 1958), 277-84.

Miscellaneous

Blau, Peter M., and Duncan, Otis Dudley. The American Occupational Structure. New York: John Wiley & Sons, Inc., 1967.

Gans, Herbert J. The Levittowners. New York: Random House, Inc., 1967.

Glick, Paul C. American Families. New York: John Wiley and Sons., 1957.

Hawley, Amos H. Human Ecology. New York: The Ronald Press Company, 1950.

Kiser, Clyde V.; Grabill, Wilson H.; and Campbell, Arthur A. Trends and Variations in Fertility in the United States. Cambridge: Harvard University Press, 1968.

Lewin, Kurt. Field Theory in Social Science. New York: Harper and Row, 1951.

Siegel, Sidney. "Level of Aspiration and Decision Making." Psychological Review, LXIV (1957), 253-62.

Wirth, Louis. The Ghetto. Chicago: University of Chicago Press, 1928. Chicago: University of Chicago Press, Phoenix Books, 1956.

Methodology

Edwards, Allen L. Experimental Design in Psychological Research. Rev. ed. New York: Holt, Rinehart and Winston, 1960.

Goodman, Leo A., and Kruskal, William H. "Measures of Association for Cross-Classifications." Journal of the American Statistical Association, XLIX (December, 1954), 732-64.

Harman, Harry H. Modern Factor Analysis. 2d ed., rev. Chicago: University of Chicago Press, 1967.

Kruskal, William H., and Wallis, W. Allen. "Use of Ranks in One-Criterion Variance Analysis." Journal of the American Statistical Association, XLVII (December, 1952), 583-621.

Wilcoxon, Frank. "Individual Comparisons by Ranking Methods." Biometrics Bulletin, I (December, 1945), 80-83.

Sources of Data

U. S. Bureau of the Census. U. S. Census of Population: 1960. Vol. I: Characteristics of the Population. Washington, D. C.: U. S. Government Printing Office, 1964.

________. U. S. Census of Population: 1960. Subject Reports. Persons by Family Characteristics. Final Report PC(2)-4B. Washington, D. C.: U. S. Government Printing Office, 1964.

________. U. S. Census of Population: 1960. Subject Reports. Sources and Structure of Family Income. Final Report PC(2)-4C. Washington, D. C.: U. S. Government Printing Office, 1964.

________. U. S. Census of Population: 1960. Subject Reports. Employment Status and Work Experience. Final Report PC(2)-6A. Washington, D. C.: U. S. Government Printing Office, 1963.

________. U. S. Censuses of Population and Housing: 1960. Census Tracts. Washington, D. C.: U. S. Government Printing Office, 1962.

THE UNIVERSITY OF CHICAGO
DEPARTMENT OF GEOGRAPHY
RESEARCH PAPERS (Lithographed, 6×9 Inches)

(*Available from Department of Geography, Rosenwald Hall, The University of Chicago, Chicago Illinois 60637. Price: $4.50 each; by series subscription, $4.00 each.*)

*1. GROSS, HERBERT HENRY. *Educational Land Use in the River Forest–Oak Park Community (Illinois)*
*2. EISEN, EDNA E. *Educational Land Use in Lake County, Ohio*
*3. WEIGEND, GUIDO GUSTAV. *The Cultural Pattern of South Tyrol (Italy)*
*4. NELSON, HOWARD JOSEPH. *The Livelihood Structure of Des Moines, Iowa*
*5. MATTHEWS, JAMES SWINTON. *Expressions of Urbanism in the Sequent Occupance of Northeastern Ohio*
*6. GINSBURG, NORTON SYDNEY. *Japanese Prewar Trade and Shipping in the Oriental Triangle*
*7. KEMLER, JOHN H. *The Struggle for Wolfram in the Iberian Peninsula, June, 1942—June, 1944: A Study in Political and Economic Geography in Wartime*
*8. PHILBRICK, ALLEN K. *The Geography of Education in the Winnetka and Bridgeport Communities of Metropolitan Chicago*
*9. BRADLEY, VIRGINIA. *Functional Patterns in the Guadalupe Counties of the Edwards Plateau*
*10. HARRIS, CHAUNCY D., and FELLMANN, JEROME DONALD. *A Union List of Geographical Serials*
*11. DE MEIRLEIR, MARCEL J. *Manufactural Occupance in the West Central Area of Chicago*
*12. FELLMANN, JEROME DONALD. *Truck Transportation Patterns of Chicago*
*13. HOTCHKISS, WESLEY AKIN. *Areal Pattern of Religious Institutions in Cincinnati*
*14. HARPER, ROBERT ALEXANDER. *Recreational Occupance of the Moraine Lake Region of Northeastern Illinois and Southeastern Wisconsin*
*15. WHEELER, JESSE HARRISON, JR. *Land Use in Greenbrier County, West Virginia*
*16. MCGAUGH, MAURICE EDRON. *The Settlement of the Saginaw Basin*
*17. WATTERSON, ARTHUR WELDON. *Economy and Land Use Patterns of McLean County, Illinois*
*18. HORBALY, WILLIAM. *Agricultural Conditions in Czechoslovakia, 1950*
*19. GUEST, BUDDY ROSS. *Resource Use and Associated Problems in the Upper Cimarron Area*
*20. SORENSEN, CLARENCE WOODROW. *The Internal Structure of the Springfield, Illinois, Urbanized Area*
*21. MUNGER, EDWIN S. *Relational Patterns of Kampala, Uganda*
*22. KHALAF, JASSIM M. *The Water Resources of the Lower Colorado River Basin*
*23. GULICK, LUTHER H. *Rural Occupance in Utuado and Jayuya Municipios, Puerto Rico*
*24. TAAFFE, EDWARD JAMES. *The Air Passenger Hinterland of Chicago*
*25. KRAUSE, ANNEMARIE ELISABETH. *Mennonite Settlement in the Paraguayan Chaco*
*26. HAMMING, EDWARD. *The Port of Milwaukee*
*27. CRAMER, ROBERT ELI. *Manufacturing Structure of the Cicero District, Metropolitan Chicago*
*28. PIERSON, WILLIAM H. *The Geography of the Bellingham Lowland, Washington*
*29. WHITE, GILBERT F. *Human Adjustment to Floods: A Geographical Approach to the Flood Problem in the United States*
30. OSBORN, DAVID G. *Geographical Features of the Automation of Industry* 1953. 120 pp.
*31. THOMAN, RICHARD S. *The Changing Occupance Pattern of the Tri-State Area, Missouri, Kansas, and Oklahoma*
*32. ERICKSEN, SHELDON D. *Occupance in the Upper Deschutes Basin, Oregon*
*33. KENYON, JAMES B. *The Industrialization of the Skokie Area*
*34. PHILLIPS, PAUL GROUNDS. *The Hashemite Kingdom of Jordan: Prolegomena to a Technical Assistance Program*
*35. CARMIN, ROBERT LEIGHTON. *Anápolis, Brazil: Regional Capital of an Agricultural Frontier*
*36. GOLD, ROBERT N. *Manufacturing Structure and Pattern of the South Bend–Mishawaka Area*
*37. SISCO, PAUL HARDEMAN. *The Retail Function of Memphis*
*38. VAN DONGEN, IRENE S. *The British East African Transport Complex*
*39. FRIEDMANN, JOHN R. P. *The Spatial Structure of Economic Development in the Tennessee Valley*
*40. GROTEWOLD, ANDREAS. *Regional Changes in Corn Production in the United States from 1909 to 1949*
*41. BJORKLUND, E. M. *Focus on Adelaide—Functional Organization of the Adelaide Region, Australia*
*42. FORD, ROBERT N. *A Resource Use Analysis and Evaluation of the Everglades Agricultural Area*
*43. CHRISTENSEN, DAVID E. *Rural Occupance in Transition: Sumter and Lee Counties, Georgia*
*44. GUZMÁN, LOUIS E. *Farming and Farmlands in Panama*

* Out of print.

*45. ZADROZNY, MITCHELL G. *Water Utilization in the Middle Mississippi Valley*
*46. AHMED, G. MUNIR. *Manufacturing Structure and Pattern of Waukegan–North Chicago*
*47. RANDALL, DARRELL. *Factors of Economic Development and the Okovango Delta*
48. BOXER, BARUCH. *Israeli Shipping and Foreign Trade* 1957. 176 pp.
*49. MAYER, HAROLD M. *The Port of Chicago and the St. Lawrence Seaway*
*50. PATTISON, WILLIAM D. *Beginnings of the American Rectangular Land Survey System, 1784–1800* 1957. 2d printing 1963. 260 pp. Available from Ohio Historical Society.
*51. BROWN, ROBERT HAROLD. *Political Areal-Functional Organization: With Special Reference to St. Cloud, Minnesota.*
52. BEYER, JACQUELYN. *Integration of Grazing and Crop Agriculture: Resources Management Problems in the Uncompahgre Valley Irrigation Project.*
53. ACKERMAN, EDWARD A. *Geography as a Fundamental Research Discipline* 1958. 40 pp. $1.00
*54. AL-KHASHAB, WAFIQ HUSSAIN. *The Water Budget of the Tigris and Euphrates Basin*
55. LARIMORE, ANN EVANS. *The Alien Town: Patterns of Settlement in Busoga, Uganda* 1958. 210 pp.
56. MURPHY, FRANCIS C. *Regulating Flood-Plain Development* 1958. 216 pp.
*57. WHITE, GILBERT F., *et al. Changes in Urban Occupance of Flood Plains in the United States*
58. COLBY, MARY MC RAE. *The Geographic Structure of Southeastern North Carolina*
*59. MEGEE, MARY CATHERINE. *Monterrey, Mexico: Internal Patterns and External Relations*
60. WEBER, DICKINSON. *A Comparison of Two Oil City Business Centers (Odessa-Midland, Texas)* 1958. 256 pp.
61. PLATT, ROBERT S. *Field Study in American Geography* 1959. 408 pp.
62. GINSBURG, NORTON, editor. *Essays on Geography and Economic Development* 1960. 196 pp.
63. HARRIS, CHAUNCY D., and FELLMANN, JEROME D. *International List of Geographical Serials* 1960. 247 pp.
*64. TAAFFE, ROBERT N. *Rail Transportation and the Economic Development of Soviet Central Asia*
*65. SHEAFFER, JOHN R. *Flood Proofing: An Element in a Flood Damage Reduction Program*
*66. RODGERS, ALLAN L. *The Industrial Geography of the Port of Genova*
67. KENYON, JAMES B. *Industrial Localization and Metropolitan Growth: The Paterson-Passaic District.* 1960. 250 pp.
68. GINSBURG, NORTON. *An Atlas of Economic Development* 1961. 119 pp. 14×8½". Cloth $7.50. University of Chicago Press.
69. CHURCH, MARTHA. *Spatial Organization of Electric Power Territories in Massachusetts* 1960. 200 pp.
70. WHITE, GILBERT F., *et al. Papers on Flood Problems* 1961. 234 pp.
71. GILBERT, E. W. *The University Town in England and West Germany* 1961. 79 pp. 4 plates. 30 maps and diagrams.
72. BOXER, BARUCH. *Ocean Shipping in the Evolution of Hong Kong* 1961. 108 pp.
*73. ROBINSON, IRA M. *New Industrial Towns of Canada's Resource Frontier* (Research Paper No. 4, Program of Education and Research in Planning, The University of Chicago.)
74. TROTTER, JOHN E. *State Park System in Illinois* 1962. 152 pp.
75. BURTON, IAN. *Types of Agricultural Occupance of Flood Plains in the United States* 1962. 167 pp.
*76. PRED, ALLAN. *The External Relations of Cities during 'Industrial Revolution'*
77. BARROWS, HARLAN H. *Lectures on the Historical Geography of the United States as Given in 1933* Edited by WILLIAM A. KOELSCH. 1962. 248 pp.
*78. KATES, ROBERT WILLIAM. *Hazard and Choice Perception in Flood Plain Management*
79. HUDSON, JAMES. *Irrigation Water Use in the Utah Valley, Utah* 1962. 249 pp.
*80. ZELINSKY, WILBUR. *A Bibliographic Guide to Population Geography*
*81. DRAINE, EDWIN H. *Import Traffic of Chicago and Its Hinterland*
*82. KOLARS, JOHN F. *Tradition, Season, and Change in a Turkish Village* NAS-NRC Foreign Field Research Program Report No. 15.
*83. WIKKRAMATILEKE, RUDOLPH. *Southeast Ceylon: Trends and Problems in Agricultural Settlement*
84. KANSKY, K. J. *Structure of Transportation Networks: Relationships between Network Geometry and Regional Characteristics* 1963. 155 pp.
*85. BERRY, BRIAN J. L. *Commercial Structure and Commercial Blight*
86. BERRY, BRIAN J. L., and TENNANT, ROBERT J. *Chicago Commercial Reference Handbook* 1963. 278 pp.
*87. BERRY, BRIAN J. L., and HANKINS, THOMAS D. *A Bibliographic Guide to the Economic Regions of the United States*
*88. MARCUS, MELVIN G. *Climate-Glacier Studies in the Juneau Ice Field Region, Alaska*
89. SMOLE, WILLIAM J. *Owner-Cultivatorship in Middle Chile* 1964. 176 pp.
90. HELVIG, MAGNE. *Chicago's External Truck Movements: Spatial Interaction between the Chicago Area and Its Hinterland*

* Out of print.

91. HILL, A. DAVID. *The Changing Landscape of a Mexican Municipio, Villa Las Rosas, Chiapas* NAS-NRC Foreign Field Research Program Report No. 26. 1964. 121 pp.
92. SIMMONS, JAMES W. *The Changing Pattern of Retail Location* 1964. 202 pp.
93. WHITE, GILBERT F. *Choice of Adjustment to Floods* 1964. 150 pp.
94. MCMANIS, DOUGLAS R. *The Initial Evaluation and Utilization of the Illinois Prairies, 1815–1840* 1964. 109 pp.
95. PERLE, EUGENE D. *The Demand for Transportation: Regional and Commodity Studies in the United States* 1964. 130 pp.
*96. HARRIS, CHAUNCY D. *Annotated World List of Selected Current Geographical Serials in English*
97. BOWDEN, LEONARD W. *Diffusion of the Decision To Irrigate: Simulation of the Spread of a New Resource Management Practice in the Colorado Northern High Plains* 1965. 146 pp.
98. KATES, ROBERT W. *Industrial Flood Losses: Damage Estimation in the Lehigh Valley* 1965. 76 pp.
99. RODER, WOLF. *The Sabi Valley Irrigation Projects* 1965. 213 pp.
100. SEWELL, W. R. DERRICK. *Water Management and Floods in the Fraser River Basin* 1965. 163 pp.
101. RAY, D. MICHAEL. *Market Potential and Economic Shadow: A Quantitative Analysis of Industrial Location in Southern Ontario* 1965. 164 pp.
102. AHMAD, QAZI. *Indian Cities: Characteristics and Correlates* 1965. 184 pp.
103. BARNUM, H. GARDINER. *Market Centers and Hinterlands in Baden-Württemberg* 1966. 172 pp.
104. SIMMONS, JAMES W. *Toronto's Changing Retail Complex* 1966. 126 pp.
105. SEWELL, W. R. DERRICK, *et al. Human Dimensions of Weather Modification* 1966. 423 pp.
106. SAARINEN, THOMAS FREDERICK. *Perception of the Drought Hazard on the Great Plains* 1966 .183 pp.
107. SOLZMAN, DAVID M. *Waterway Industrial Sites: A Chicago Case Study* 1967. 138 pp.
108. KASPERSON, ROGER E. *The Dodecanese: Diversity and Unity in Island Politics* 1967. 184 pp.
109. LOWENTHAL, DAVID, editor. *Environmental Perception and Behavior* 1967. 88 pp.
110. REED, WALLACE E. *Areal Interaction in India: Commodity Flows of the Bengal-Bihar Industrial Area* 1967. 210 pp.
*111. BERRY, BRIAN J. L. *Essays on Commodity Flows and the Spatial Structure of the Indian Economy*
112. BOURNE, LARRY S. *Private Redevelopment of the Central City, Spatial Processes of Structural Change in the City of Toronto* 1967. 199 pp.
113. BRUSH, JOHN E., and GAUTHIER, HOWARD L., JR. *Service Centers and Consumer Trips: Studies on the Philadelphia Metropolitan Fringe* 1968. 182 pp.
114. CLARKSON, JAMES D. *The Cultural Ecology of a Chinese Village, Cameron Highlands, Malaysia* 1968. 174 pp.
115. BURTON, IAN, KATES, ROBERT W., and SNEAD, RODMAN E. *The Human Ecology of Coastal Flood Hazard in Megalopolis* 1968. 196 pp.
116. MURDIE, ROBERT, *Factorial Ecology of Metropolitan Toronto, 1951–1961* 1968. 212 pp.
117. WONG, SHUE TUCK, *Perception of Choice and Factors Affecting Industrial Water Supply Decisions in Northeastern Illinois* 1968. 96 pp.
118. JOHNSON, DOUGLAS. *The Nature of Nomadism: A Comparative Study of Pastoral Migrations in Northern Africa and Southwestern Asia* 1969. 200 pp.
119. DIENES, LESLIE. *Locational Factors and Locational Developments in the Soviet Chemical Industry* 1969. 285 pp.
120. MIHELIC, DUSAN. *The Political Element in the Port Geography of Trieste* 1969. 104 pp.
121. BAUMANN, DUANE. *The Recreational Use of Domestic Water Supply Reservoir: Perception and Choice* 1969. 125 pp.
122. LIND, AULIS O. *Coastal Landforms of Cat Island, Bahamas: A Study of Holocene Accretionary Topography and Sea-Level Change* 1969. 156 pp.
123. WHITNEY, JOSEPH. *China: Area, Administration and Nation Building* 1970. 198 pp.
124. EARICKSON, ROBERT. *The Spatial Behavior of Hospital Patients: A Behavioral Approach to Spatial Interaction in Metropolitan Chicago.* 1970. 198 pp.
125. DAY, JOHN CHADWICK. *Managing the Lower Rio Grande: An Experience in International River Development.* 1970 (in press)
126. MACIVER, IAN. *Urban Water Supply Alternatives: Perception and Choice in the Grand Basin Ontario.* 1970. 178 pp.
127. GOHEEN, PETER G., *Victorian Toronto, 1850 to 1900: Pattern and Process of Growth* 1970. 278 pp.
128. GOOD, CHARLES M. *Rural Markets and Trade in East Africa* 1970. 252 pp.
129. MEYER, DAVID R. *Spatial Variation of Black Urban Households* 1970. 127 pp

* Out of print.